SURVIVING THE WARZONE

Brooklyn

SURVIVING THE WARZONE

Growing Up East New York

To: Pat-Raul

Richard ⊕

2017

Richard G Quarantello

To order additional copies of this book, contact:
Xlibris
1-888-795-4274
www.Xlibris.com
Orders@Xlibris.com
549855

I dedicate this book to My daughter Alyse, My son Richard, My son Gregory, Mr. Nero and my wife Wendi for putting up with me for five years in Costa Rica while I wrote this book, Steven Strickman (Hi Ho) as he was the ambassador of East New York.

Stories in Order of Year

THIS STORY

The story I am about to tell you is true. It's the story of a little-known village, its good and bad times. We begin with the original settlers of the land—the Native Americans with over five hundred years of history, before the Europeans came to the place known as New York City. It had been the home of the Algonquian language group. Literally, hundreds of these self-governing bands lived along the east coast, from North Carolina to Canada, and at least eighteen of them lived in the New York City area. The Canarsies were especially prominent in what is now Brooklyn. Although these local groups were not as advanced as the Maya, Inca, or Aztec nations, they lived in peace with nature and with one another. In 1624, the Dutch East India Company established the first permanent European settlement in what is now New York City. Dutch farmers moved across the East River to Brooklyn in order to cultivate new farmlands. Land was plentiful, and they settled in areas like Flatbush and moved east to Canarsie, Brownville, and East New York, the very east end of Brooklyn, the gateway to Long Island. The Dutch built churches, small towns, and roads. I remember the Old Dutch Reform Church on New Lots and Schenck Avenue, with its adjoining graveyard with the names of many of the original Dutch settlers, and still now street names like Van Siclen and Lott family's the Hopkins, Cozine and many more prominent families of the time, which still exist today. The arrival of the English in 1664 annexed Dutch control. In 1776, a new nation was born. The continental army under George Washington in the Battle of Long Island against the British and Hessian forces fortified passes along a section of Flatbush Avenue, which became Prospect Park a century later. With the rest of his troops, he took and fortified the higher ground at Brooklyn Heights, with his back to the East River. Ever since I could remember, I loved American history. As a young man, I would walk these areas of Brooklyn and think and picture that this was once an all-wooded area with trees and

---

11

streams and that our great nation was born here. The Americans won their war of independence in 1783. A few years before 1890, the town of New Lots, part of Kings County, was much like other towns of the state, having a central village surrounded by land on which the farmers raised produce for the market. Dirt roads were common; some streets were paved with cobblestones. I remember the first cobblestoned streets I saw when I was a boy were on Livonia Avenue under the IRT train teasel. East New York at the turn of the century quickly became metropolitan. The old mill situated at the foot of Crescent Street was always a landmark for farmers and fisherman. I remember the little wooden bridge and the small row of homes standing on piles a few feet above the old mill marsh, surrounded by cattails. I heard Old Dutch, German, and Polish squatters lived in these small old wooden homes. I remember my friends and I were afraid to go near those homes. We called it ghost town. After World War II came the individual social responsibilities of the 1950s. East New York by the 1950s was going through peace and prosperity like the rest of the country, manifested by a positive family life. I didn't know I was poor; all I knew was those magical years of domestic tranquility. I remember those great times as a young boy with my own childlike problems like which games are me and my friends going to play after school, such as stickball, hide-and-seek, kick the can, Johnny on the pony, war, hot beans, cops and robbers down the alleyways between the buildings and the backyards. Other games were street hockey, Chinese handball, box ball, stoopball, red light green light, pitch the penny, punchball, ringolevio, and roller skating. We made our own scooters out of two-by-four wooden milk crates and one roller skate. My personal favorite game was skelly. Every summer, on practically every block in East New York, the kids would open the johnny pumps (fire hydrants) to keep cool from those hot and humid days. I would play games with my friends for hours till I was called in for super. My father had this loud whistle, and when I heard that whistle, I would stop playing and run home for supper. Baseball and football were played in vacant lots. These games were handed down by our older brothers and sisters. I felt safe on the streets, and I made longtime friendships. In the 1950s, most of the residents were chiefly Italians, Jews, Irish, and Negroes. Almost everyone was in the same economic situation. I remember before the 1960 people were warm, friendly, and helpful. Most of my friends were second-generation Italian Americans. My grandparents were from Naples, Italy. They came to America just before the turn of the twentieth century, with aunts, uncles, and cousins living in the same neighborhood, within a few minutes' walking distance from one another. Do something wrong in the neighborhood, and you will hear about it when you get home from school, with those famous words "wait till your father gets home." From the new political hacks to the young idealists, the 1960s were about to change this country's perspective. For the young idealists, it was about war and peace, civil rights, and Vietnam. The politician's motivation was to secure their place in history, their misguided sense of power. ("Power always sincerely, conscientiously believes itself right. Power always thinks it has a great soul and vast view, beyond the comprehension of the weak, letter from John Adams to Thomas Jefferson, February 2, 1816.) In the 1960s, East New York, Brooklyn, made the Wild West look like Disney World. East New York was lawless! Street gangs dominated Brooklyn. The white gangs took street names like the New Lots Boys, Fulton and Rockaway, the Crescents, Liberty Park Boys, Fountain and Pitkin, and Hemlock and Sutter. The black and Puerto Rican gangs took cool names, like the Chaplains, the largest black gang in Brooklyn. There were the Mau Maus, the Bishops, the El Quintos, the Roman Lords and the El Tones, the largest Puerto Rican gang in East New York. The Puerto Rican gangs and the black gangs didn't like one another and would go to war. However, they would join forces when they went to war with the white gangs. We fought for one basic reason: to keep our simple way of life. One such gang in East New York was the New Lots Boys. The New Lots Boys go back before the 1930s and were mostly Italian and Jewish, with a few Irish and Puerto Rican guys. I was ten years old when I first heard about the New Lots Boys. There was a fight in my school, PS 202, between an Italian guy named Tony Cuccia and a black guy named Herbie Randell, the toughest guy in my school. I didn't know any of the New Lots Boys; all I heard was that they were one tough gang. Tony Cuccia beat Herbie Randell really bad. I felt this unknown sense of pride. They were the toughest-looking guys I have ever seen. I wanted to learn how to fight like that.

My uncle Frank had a Butcher shop on the corner of New Lots Avenue and Elton Street. As a young boy, I loved to go to New Lots Avenue with my mother. Sometimes, we would take the train to downtown Brooklyn to go clothes shopping at A&S and May's. For the holidays like Christmas and Easter, we shopped for formal clothes for men and boys at Buddy Lee. We would take the IRT train, which ran above Lavonia Avenue. We would get on the train at the Triangle, the heart of the New Lots Boys hangout. I lived on Elton Street south of Linden Boulevard. Mom and I would walk north on Elton Street and have to pass Elton Street Park where all the young New Lots Boys and girls would hang out. I had heard stories about how bad the New Lots Boys were, with their cool motorcycle jackets and slicked-back, DA (Ducks Ass) hair. The younger guys in the park looked and dressed exactly like the big guys. It was 1955. I didn't know about or even think of being in a street gang. I saw movies like *Blackboard Jungle* and *The Wild Ones*; that wasn't me. I was a very shy, skinny, and quiet kid, just wanting to play outdoor games or play with my army soldiers on my mother's kitchen floor. When I turned eleven years old, I asked my uncle Frank if I could work in his butcher shop as a delivery boy. He told me he would give me a job when I turn twelve years old. Before that, I would collect soda bottles from the new construction sites, shine shoes, or deliver circulars for the Speed Way supper market. It was 1957. I was twelve years old and had my first real steady job. Every day after school from 3:30 p.m. till 6:00 p.m., on Fridays till 9:00 p.m., and on Saturdays from 6:00 a.m. till 6:00 p.m., I would ride the big butcher bike with that large basket in the front, making meat delivery all around East New York and Brownsville for ten dollars a week plus tips. I was so happy to have a job. Every day on my way to work, I had to pass by the Elton Street Park where the young New Lots Boys and girls hung out. They were all so nice, and the girls were cute as hell. I knew a few of the guys from school, so when I would ride the butcher bike pass the park, I would stop at the park and talk to some of the guys I knew, and that's where my journey began. It was 1958. I was thirteen years old and in a gang, with a DA hairdo, a leather jacket, and maybe the attitude. One of my now new friends, Anthony, was being trained in boxing at Elton Street Park. He was a handsome black man, about five feet six, with huge arms. He was quick and always wearing a cap tilled on the right side of his head. He looked tough. I was still a little shy, but I wanted to learn how to box. I was a strong kid, and riding the butcher bike and lifting weights in my basement for a year put me in good shape. I was so desperate to learn how to box, so I ask Anthony to introduce me to the park man. Everyone called him Mr. Nero. He was well respected by the people in the neighborhood and the New Lots Boys, that said a lot about Mr. Nero because the guys in the park abused every park man before Mr. Nero got there.

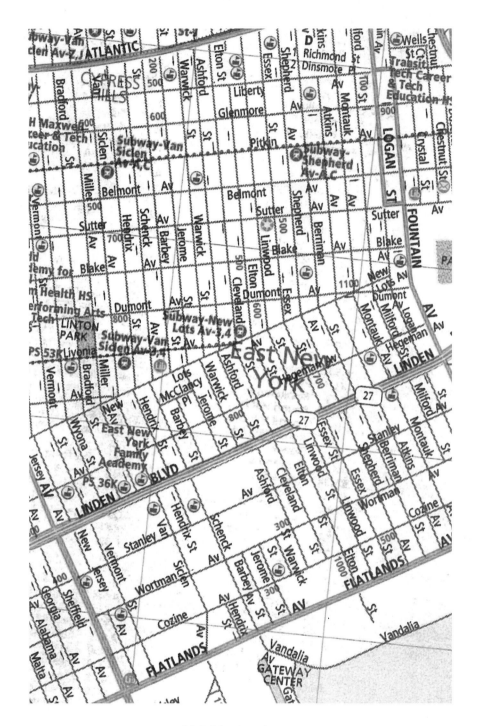

Neighborhood map

New Lots Boy
Meets Mr. Nero

I remember it was a warm spring day. Mr. Nero was racking up leafs in front of the park house. The park house was a small brick building on the Linwood Street side of the park, with an office and a storage area in the middle. The girl's bathroom was on the right side and the boy's bathroom was on the left side of the building. I remember being so nervous. He looked so cool and moved like a big cat in the jungle. Thinking I want to move like that, I finally got the nerve to talk to him and introduce myself. I didn't think he knew me. When I introduced myself, I was so surprised he knew who I was. You're Richie Q. I see you ride around on that big bike for your uncle every day. I like to see young people working. It builds character. I couldn't believe he noticed me. He was so easy to talk to. He was over twenty years older than I was, and I was now finding myself very comfortable talking to him. I asked Mr. Nero if he can teach me how to fight. He stood there for a second, looking strong and charismatic, and I felt something was wrong. He said, "Lesson number one, it's not called fighting, it's called boxing, and it's a science. Fighting is a reaction to your emotion; boxing is thinking using your mind. It's an art that will make and shape your character." I stood there thinking this man is talking to me as if I was his equal. I can't tell you how proud that made me feel. He told me to come to the park house after school for a half-hour lesson before I went to work. I began training with Mr. Nero religiously, never missing one day. The man became my mentor and best friend. I saw my father get up early every morning and go to work, never missing a day no matter what the weather was. I believe this gave me a good work ethic. At a very young age, I chose to work, learn, and train hard for Mr. Nero instead of playing handball, stickball, or punchball with my friends. I had lessons to learn. Mr. Nero was training my friend Anthony for about a year. After training for two weeks, he had Anthony Stablie and me put on twelve-ounce gloves and spar. In less than a few seconds, I hit Anthony with a right-hand body shot; he doubled up and hit the park house floor. After a year of training with Mr. Nero and working out in my cousin Tony's garage hitting the heavy bag, which Mr. Nero showed me how to make using an army duffel bag, old rugs, half an old car tire tube, and sand. Mr. Nero gave me not only my new physical skills but also life lessons when speaking to me, which they don't teach young men in school. Mr. Nero once told me that if I wanted to keep a good attitude, I should value the people that make a good impact in my life and use my mind and emotions to favor my skills. At fourteen years old, I was loving life. Mr. Nero taught me how to think. I learned at this young age short survival lessons, like how to listen, watch, stay quiet, and stay back. I always knew when it was time to act. I continued to work hard at my new skills and grow. My father would always tell me to get a good city job with benefits and a pension. Mr. Nero would tell me that when we are young, we all have self-doubt. Self-confidence will come with knowledge and by working hard at your skills. Mr. Nero would meet me sometimes at my uncle's butcher shop for lunch. We would go across the street to Benny's Luncheonette, have a great lunch and wash it down with a Dr. Brown's Cel-Ray soda, have some good laughs, and talk. I loved hearing his lessons. We would go to the gold gloves every-year. He took me to Madison Square Garden to see Sugar Ray Robinson versus Joey Archie. That time, Sugar Ray was forty-two years old. I got to see the greatest. We also went to see one of the three boxing matches of Emil Griffin versus Nino Benvenuti. We spend a lot of great time in those days, and he taught me the things that matter: to explore my dreams. But I was now blinded and naive to the worst kind of bad. Here is my journey.

Mom and Dad

My mom and dad met at a small park on Schermerhorn Street downtown Brooklyn. He told me that he and his friend Sal were walking past the park when he saw this really cute young lady sitting on a park bench. He told his friend Sal to wait just a minute because he just spotted his future wife and walked into the park. He told me there she was, sitting with her legs crossed looking like an angel, with a starched white blouse, a pleated navy blue skirt, and shiny black pattern leather shoes with white socks. As he got closer to her, he could see her hazel cat eyes, her sparkling clean light brown hair that he knew smelled as good as it looked, her silky white face, and her gorgeous legs. He was in love. My dad was also very handsome. He stood about five feet nine at about one hundred and fifty pounds, with dark brown eyes, black hair, and fair complexion. He wore a pair of tan pleated slacks, a brown belt, a pair of brown shoes, and a short-sleeved off-white tailored shirt. There was only one problem. There she was, sitting like Snow White waiting for her knight to arrive, and her left hand was holding a baby carriage. Dad maybe a little shy or afraid, but with this deep unsteady voice, he asked if that was her baby. Without raising her head just her beautiful eyes and with a soft warm smile, she said the baby was her sister Fanny's. That baby was my cousin Sonny. He asked her on a date. She turned, looked away, and took a deep breath. My dad said his stomach was in knots. She turned back and said that he would have to come to her house to pick her up and to meet her parents. A peaceful silence came over them, and she asked him if he would like to sit. He struggled to get his weakened legs to move. Dad's friend, Sal, smiled and waved good-bye. A few years later, a New Lots boy was conceived.

New Lots Boy
versus New Car Man

It was the summer of 1959. I was fourteen years old. It was a Saturday, and I had just finished my work day at my Uncle Frank's butcher shop. It had been a beautiful summer's day, and I had money in my pocket. I was feeling good. I had asked my uncle if I could leave fifteen minutes early so I could run up to Blake Avenue, to the only men's fashion store in our area. I jumped on my bike and raced to the store. It was on the south side of Blake Avenue in the middle of the block, between Elton and Cleveland Streets. I got to the store with ten minutes to spare before it closed.

I was a good customer, and the owner, an older Jewish man with a slight European accent, was always very pleasant. He told me to settle down and bring my bike inside the store because we both knew without having to say it that East New York was on a fast track to losing its soul. He knew that I was a clotheshorse, so before I could say a word, he told me to look around and went into the back room where he kept his stock and received new goods. After a few minutes, he came out holding in his hands something which to me looked like the holy grail of vests. As he walked toward me, it seemed like slow motion; and as he got closer, I could see the front of the vest was this wonderful soft moss green wide corduroy. The buttons on the front were kind of an amber-colored bone. As he came up to me, I could see the back of the vest was a black satin material with a small belt and a silver buckle.

What a salesman; he knew that now I would need the whole nine yards. Next, he presented these cotton black chino pants, also with a small belt in the back with a silver buckle. He told me to look at some shirts while he turned and headed for the back room again. I found the perfect cotton short-sleeved shirt—a red, black, with a moss green paisley design with a button-down collar. In those days, I always buttoned my shirts to the top neck button. Then the owner came out with a shoe box in his hand. As he was walking toward me, I had this great feeling of expectation. He began to open the lid of the box, and with a big smile on his face, he reached in with his right hand and pulled out a unique pair of ankle-high suede desert boots. The thing that made them unique was their color. I had only seen desert boots in tan, but those boots were all black, even the gum soles and laces were black. He knew my size, and to show how much the owner knew me, in the shoe box was a new pair of socks and a pair of men's garters. I always wore men's garters to hold up my socks. The owner looked at me with a big smile and said to me in his slight Old World accent, "I've never seen anyone of my customers get as much pleasure as you do in my store." I told him I loved to get dressed for the ladies. He thought that was so funny, and he laughed so hard. He went behind the counter to cash me out. Then he bent down and put a small bottle of Canoe Cologne on the counter and said, "This is for you. The young ladies like it. No charge." We had a good laugh.

I couldn't get home fast enough. When I got home, my mother was making dinner. I called my friend Charlie P from Montauk Avenue. Charlie and the crew from Montauk Avenue, at about that time, became New Lots Boys, along with Mike Mcgrane (nickname the Mick) and the crew from PS 202 school yard. So Charlie and I made plans to go out. I ironed my new clothes, took a shower, had a light dinner, and got dressed. I was feeling, looking, and smelling good; after all, I had just put on half a bottle of Canoe. I threw my white short brim fedora on, with its black band and white pearl in the front. I yelled "bye, Mom," and I was gone. From my house, Charlie's house was about three-quarters of a mile. Charlie lived on the south side of Blake Avenue, between Atkins and Montauk Avenues, in a two-story attached house, in the second-floor apartment. Charlie was about my size at that time. He was five feet nine and about one hundred and forty pounds, with thick black hair combed back into a DA with a pompadour in front, dark brown eyes, and light olive complexion. He was also dressed to kill, with a red short-sleeved shirt, a pair of black slacks, and a pair of new spit-shine featherweight shoes, and smelled like he took a bath in a gallon of Canoe. Charlie didn't have a problem with the young ladies. It took me about a half an hour to walk there. Charlie met me at Leo's, a small luncheonette on Montauk Avenue and a few feet south of the corner from Blake Avenue. We thought of going to the PS 202 school yard; there were always cute girls there. We walked to the corner of Blake and Montauk Avenues and then made a left toward Atkins Avenue. As we got to the middle of Blake Avenue, Charlie stepped into the street and turned to yell up to his mom that he'd be home late. Just then, a new 1959 Plymouth drove by and tried to hit Charlie. Charlie ran to the sidewalk just in time. We turned and yelled, "You, motherfucker!" The car stopped short on the corner. The door opened, and an older dude around twenty years old jumped out and yelled, "Who are you two punks calling a motherfucker?" Before I could say a word, he ran at me, grabbed me by my new vest, and ripped it off me. He was tall and thin, with dark greased slicked-back hair, a white short-sleeved shirt, a blue tie, and a pair of black pants. There he was, standing in the street with the front of my vest in his hands. The back of the vest fell to the ground. I ran forward, throwing three straight right hands. I hit that piece of shit so hard that I laid him out in the middle of the street, reduced to helplessness. His new car was on the corner, with the door open and the engine still running. I was so upset about my brand-new vest, and as badly as I wanted to take his car and run it up a telephone pole, like some of my friends would have done, I resisted. It was not in my character.

The streets were empty, so I picked up the front and the back of my vest. Charlie was laughing and told me that his mother could sew the vest back together. We went up and told his mother what had happened. We all went to the front of the apartment to look out the window and see what was going on with that dope. Some guy had helped him up and sat him in his car. Luckily, the vest had ripped on the seams, between the corduroy and the black satin, and Charlie's mother, a sweet gray-haired Italian woman, put it right back together. I was so happy.

After a glass of water, we went back to the window, and the car was gone. Charlie and I went outside, took a left, then made another left, south on Atkins Avenue, and walked three blocks to the PS 202 school yard. It was a beautiful night, and the school yard was packed with guys and girls; some of the prettiest girls from East New York came from that school. As soon as we walked into the school yard, we saw two guys fighting. As we tried to pass them to get to the middle of the school yard where everyone was hanging out, wouldn't you know it, one of those dudes that were fighting ran up to me and tried to grab me. I spun him around and threw him against the side of the school steps. He stopped, looked at me, and said, "Who are you?" Everyone ran toward us and said, "Don't hit him! He's drunk!" He had stopped fighting, so I let him go and told him to sit on the school yard steps and chill. His name was Raul, a good-looking guy about five feet ten and thick with a good muscle tone. It was hard to tell if he was light black or PR (Puerto Ricans) mix. The guy he was fighting with was his best friend Nino, about my size, with dark hair and dark eyes. He was an Italian guy from Italy. Raul's shirt was torn, and his friend Nino had a bloody nose. Later on, we became good friends. I told Charlie I was done and going home. As I began walking out on the Berriman Street side of the school, one of the most beautiful young ladies I have ever seen was standing in the entrance.

With a light warm breeze blowing through her long dark hair, she turned to look at me. Her eyes looked black in the moonlight, and she smiled with pearly white teeth that sparkled against her dark complexion. I looked at her and knew I was in love. I knew we would see each other again, so I forced a smile and walked away. That night, I felt like a good knight; too bad the Holy Grail of vests never gave me that profound ecstasy I was looking for from the ladies.

New Lots Boys versus Canarsie Chaplains: Round 1

It was 1959. Miles Shoes store was located on Linden Boulevard and Ashford Street, on the southeast corner. It was a pretty large store. The front of the store was all glass, and it was brightly lit at night. Across Ashford Street, the Boulevard Projects stared. It was a beautiful, warm summer Friday night. There was a party in the building across the street from the shoe store. A black gang from Canarsie called the Chaplains were at the party; there were at least twenty-five or thirty guys, and as many girls, aged about fourteen to eighteen years. Spirits were the big high back then at parties, from Piels, Rheingold, and Schaefer beer to half-and-half or jive seven; any wine would do, and marijuana was just starting to be used by teens at that time. The party later on landed in the street and half in front of the shoe store. The Chaplains were drunk and fucking with everyone that crossed their path. The employees and customers in the shoe store, both black and white, were afraid and locked the doors. I don't remember who, but one of our guys came running to the Triangle yelling that there were Chaplains fucking with people on Linden Boulevard. There were about twenty of us younger guys hanging out at the Triangle and the East New York Boy's Club across the street. At that time, we younger guys were like fourteen and fifteen years old. The Chaplains were our arch enemies, and if we had a chance to kick some Chaplains' ass, we wouldn't pass it up. On the northeast corner of Linden Boulevard was a vacant lot with a huge hole you had to go down into, about fifteen feet. The kids in the neighborhood would play baseball or football there. After the Christmas holidays, all us guys would go around the neighborhood and pick up all the Christmas trees that people would throw out to the curb. We would meet at the vacant lot on Linden Boulevard and Ashford Street, put as many of the trees that we collected into a huge pile, which were very dry by then, and light it up. It just seemed to stretch and touch the nighttime snow clouds.

We ran to Linden Boulevard. I told all the guys to wait in the lot so they wouldn't be seen, then a couple of the guys and I came up from the hole and walked into the middle of Linden Boulevard, which was a six-lane road that went through East New York and Brownsville and ended in Flatbush. As we began walking to the other side of the boulevard, we started to call out the bros. They looked at us and probably thought we were nuts, and the employees and customers in the shoe store were probably thinking the same thing. We were outnumbered about six to one. The bros began to run into the street and after us, and the bros at the party also started after us. Now they were in hot pursuit, trying to impress their ladies by kicking a few fag white boys' asses. It was a pretty busy night, and there was a lot of traffic, even on the two service roads. We backed off, and they kept coming. We made it back to the other side of the boulevard, dodging the traffic. The bros were now halfway in the middle of the boulevard when all our guys came running from the lot. Mouse had a pistol and fired a couple of shots. The bros turned back to run, dodging traffic and bullets. They couldn't get out of their own way. We could see the people in the shoe store cheering us on. We caught up to a few of the slower bros and laid them out in the middle of Linden Boulevard. The rest kept going. I imagine they didn't stop until they got back to the Canarsie Project, about a couple of miles from the party. They left their women behind in the street. If any of us had ever left our women behind, and I don't care what the numbers were, we wouldn't dare to show our faces on New Lots again; at best, you would be creeped out, meaning no one would talk to you, or you would have to take a smack and be told to stay the fuck off New Lots Avenue.

We ran up to the building where the party was at. The young ladies were all dressed and pretty shaken up. I said, "Don't worry, girls. You're fine, but this isn't right, your guys leaving you here." They said, "Tell us about it." We turned to leave, and standing right in front of me in an off-white lace dress was one of the prettiest girls I had ever seen. Her skin was blue black and smooth as silk, her hair was shinny and very short. I couldn't take my eyes off her. Her eyes were almond shaped, and against her pretty off-white dress, I knew, from my point of view, this young lady was God's work of art. The good thing about that night was that I never forgot seeing such a perfect creature. I was old enough to appreciate her beauty and too young to say what I was feeling. As we began to walk back to New Lots, the people that were in the shoe store were now outside thanking us and shaking our hands. It was a good night. My actions created an emotion in me, and that night, good everlasting dreams were created. I thank God.

New Lots Boys versus Richie Square Talk's Crew

It was 1959. This was my first fair fight, my real war. I turned fourteen years old. I was done with my work in the butcher shop and had walked down to Elton Street Park where a few of the New Lots Boys and girls were hanging out. It was cold and getting dark. I had my eye on this really cute Italian girl named Carol D, wishing she was at the park, but she had just left to go home. It was cold, and I thought maybe I'll go home and my mother would whip up a nice hot plate of macaroni when a few of our guys ran in the park. They told us that the guys from a candy store on Elton Street and Dumont Avenue fucked up a couple of our guys and they were going back. I'm down. I had been training with Mr. Nero close to a year and riding that big ass bike from Canarsie and Brownsville to Ozone Queens every day.

We've been in a couple of gang wars with the Liberty tots from Liberty Park, but they were mostly a lot of talk. I have yet to have a one-on-one, and I had no clue this would be the night. We came up with about twenty guys, way more than enough. I passed this candy store almost every day; it was only a block away from the butcher shop. I never saw more than five or eight guys hanging out there. I would sometimes stop in the candy store and have an egg cream. I got to know the owner, Benny. He was a little on the heavy side with a bad toupee. He made the best egg creams, and we became friends. He was such a pleasant man. I met him years later and he remembered me. He still had that nice way about him. You couldn't help but like him.

Between the butcher shop and Benny's candy store, there was an orphanage that I think was for Jewish children only. I knew two of these children, Ann, who was in one of my classes, and Jeff. They were nice kids. As a matter of fact, I never saw or heard the orphanage every having a problem. We walked to the corner of Elton Street and Dumont Avenue, and we all went into the candy store. At the counter, there were six of these dudes. They turned when we came in. There were twenty of us, and these guys didn't seem to be afraid. Benny said, in this real nervous stutter, to please take it outside. I was at the entrance of the store and I didn't want to upset Benny, so I told the guys let's take it outside. Our guys turned and walked out. We waited for these guys to come out. They had balls, and here they are right behind us. No sooner had I turned around than this one dude Richie Square Talk was in my face. I said to myself, "Why me? Did he think I was the leader because I said to take it outside?"

This guy was maybe a year or two older than me, about my height and weight, with a cool black leather motorcycle jacket and boots and greased pushed back hair with a pompadour in the front and a DA in the back. Now he's right in my face with a cigarette in his mouth. He took out the cigarette with his right hand and blew smoke in my face. Mr. Nero was my mentor; he not only showed me how to box but also taught me precious life lessons. When he would speak to me, I would hang on his every word. He told me once that there is only action or inaction, which one do you choose to live with? He also told me you have to work hard to be good. I never wanted to disappoint Mr. Nero.

I worked hard to be good, and he told me once he could tell I had pure spirit. At the moment the smoke hit my face, I right handed this dude, and he dropped like a bowling pin. There he was, laid out cold. I thought maybe he had something because of the way he came at me. My friends are in shock, like, "Holy shit, one shot!" I just found I knew how to do this, and I liked it. One of the older guys from New Lots, Tony lived next door from the candy store. He came outside. He was a friend of my friend Sally V's older brother, Richie, so he asked Sally who his guy was. Sally said with pride, "The guy standing." I looked at Richie Square Talk's crew, and for the first time, I felt deeply connected as I said "New Lots, motherfucker!" We all went to the Triangle. I was still hungry and ordered a vanilla malt and a beautiful greasy cheese burger and fries. The next day was Friday. After school, I went to see Mr. Nero for my lesson before I went to work at the butcher shop. I wanted to tell Mr. Nero about the fight last night, yet I didn't want him to be disappointed in me. We never talked about any of my street wars. I knew he knew from my friends and never said a word. We did not communicate these events with words. I believe we communicated with feelings. I didn't have a clue about who I was or how life works. What I did know was that my life at that moment gave me joy and pleasure, and all I knew was that my sun was rising.

New Lots Boys
versus Larkey Stompers

It was 1960. I went to East New York Vocational High School, where there were gang-related problems every day. It was an all-boys high school. Everyone in school was bad a ass, and even if you weren't, you would have to act like you were a bad ass to keep everyone else off balance. You had to watch your back in school or outside school or when walking home through some of the worst areas in East New York. There were only a few New Lots Boys that went to East New York Vocational High School, Lee F, Frankie B, Patsy P, Johnny Reb, and Richie Q (that's me), and a few of the Liberty park guys, like Tommy R and Eddie M. The good thing was that everyone had heart, and most of the other gangs in school wouldn't fuck with us, unless they cornered you alone or if they had the numbers. There was always some crew that had to test us.

East New York Vocational High School provided education to teach job-specific skills and a secondary education in learning. Your grades in grade school will determine if you will go to a liberal arts school or to a trade school. So far, it was not a bad idea, until again the city government got involved and made city vocational schools juvenile detention facilities, dumping on us once again. East New York vocational was located on Fountain Avenue, between Atlantic and Liberty Avenues. Most of the students were black and Puerto Rican. One day, while in school, I had to go to the restroom. I went and did my business, and as I turned around to go wash my hands, two Puerto Rican guys were blocking the exit door. Two more guys came in, and one of them said, "Hey, motherfucker, are you from New Lots?" I said, "Ya, motherfucker, now get the fuck out of my way, you piece of shit." As soon as I said that, this Puerto Rican guy I knew from grade school PS 202, Eddie T, walked in and said, "Maticon, you fuck with him, you fuck with me." They told Eddie to mind his own fucking business, and he said, "This is my business, mi amigo." I said, "Now let's see what kind of balls you got."

For that second, no one said a thing. Eddie and I walked out. I thanked Eddie and said, "If you have a problem with these guys, let me know." He looked at me and said with a really serious face, "Watch your back, Richie! They carry knives and will fuck you up if they get the chance." I said, "Thanks again for the heads-up." A few days went by without a problem, only some stares and bad looks, but I still knew there was going to be trouble. I hadn't heard anything, so I went about my day and kept in my fight mode, with a light breakfast of two soft-boiled eggs and one dry piece of toast, and I even had a lighter lunch and naturally wore my fight gear. This one day, my last class was on the third floor. When the class was over, I went into the hallway. Frankie B and Patsy P were also walking out of their classroom, which was right across from mine. They asked me if I had heard anything. I said, "No, but a few of these dudes are in my classes." They said, "Ya, there are a few PRs in our classes too." We went to the exit and headed downstairs. The school's staircases were concrete and steel. Once you entered the stairwell, there was no way out. We knew it was the worst place to get caught, but we had no choice. Now Frankie and Patsy had balls, most of the time too many, like way over the top. I knew if anything was going to happen with these two, someone was going to get damaged. As we began to walk down, five or six PRs were coming up and stopped on the landing in front of us. We stopped in the middle of the stairwell. The next thing I heard was the door we just came out of opened, and another five or six PRs walked onto that landing above us. Now we were stuck in the middle of the stairwell. You have to remember, the weapons of choice in the early 1960s were knives, chains, bats, car aerials, machetes, homemade zip guns, and small-caliber pistols. At that time, there was an escalation of gang violence in New York, and East New York was at the very top of the list. By mid-1960s, street warfare was normal, shootings and stabbings were commonplace, and designer drugs were on the rise. Gangs in general were created for a variety of reasons, including a sense of community or family to protect their turf. The more organized gangs operated illegal businesses and focused on personal profit rather than social issues.

Man, did I know this wasn't going to be good for us. This guy from the bottom landing said, "Are you motherfuckers from New Lots?" To my pleasant surprise and without a word, Patsy pulled out a pistol and Frankie pulled out two switchblades. I grabbed one switchblade off Frankie and said, "That's right, motherfucker, New Lots!" We walked down to the landing. I had the knife in my left hand. I cracked the first motherfucker with a straight right hand while I was still walking, and he hit the back wall. Patsy held the gun on the guys on the top landing as Frankie and I kept walking. I could hear Patsy say, "Come on, motherfucker, do me a favor." They spread out and let us by without a word. We went out the Fountain Avenue side of the school and walked home without a problem. After that incident, no one fucked with us in school.

Not long after, Frankie and Patsy left school. I transferred to Thomas Jefferson on Pennsylvania Avenue. A couple of months after that, Jefferson and I were done with. At the age of fifteen years, I never went back to school. I was still working for my uncle in the butcher shop, now full time. I loved to work, and it put honest money in my pocket. I had been out of school for only a week. It was a Friday morning when I told my uncle I was taking a walk to Blake Avenue to buy a couple of pairs of work dungarees (jeans). The store was on the corner of Elton Street and Blake Avenue. As I walked out of the store and started to walk down Elton Street to go to work, two PRs came up behind me. They said, "Hey, New Lots, what do you got in the bag?" I said, as I stepped forward with the bag in my left hand, "I got dungarees." I said, "Here, you want to see, scumbag?" I extended my left hand with the bag in it, and as he went to grab the bag, I threw a quick overhand right, catching him perfectly. He didn't go down, but I could feel I had broken his nose. He staggered back, turned, and ran. The moment I hit the one guy, the other guy grabbed me low, knocking me back off my feet. He wasn't a big guy; he was about my size. As I went down, I pulled him down with me. I held him close to me with my left hand and bit his face. He was pretty strong and was trying hard to get up. I held him down and threw at least ten short right hands to his face and jaw. He was done; he never threw a punch. I left him there facedown and bleeding, got up, picked up my bag, and walked back to work. I went into the butcher shop, put the bag in the back, and put on a freshly starched white apron. In the store were two old Italian lady customers, with their mostly gray hair, long black dresses, and grocery pull carts, my uncle, and Richie R, a friend of mine who also worked there in the shop. As I was coming out of the back room, the guy that I had just beaten up ran in the shop. The butcher shop was on the southeast corner of Elton Street and New Lots Avenue. It had one huge picture window facing New Lots Avenue and a smaller window facing Elton Street. People entered the store from New Lots Avenue. There was an old wooden floor that we covered with sawdust. As you entered the shop, there was a grocery shelf on the right and white porcelain and glass meat cases on the left and rear of the store. He came running into the butcher shop wailing a machete and yelling "I want Richie!" The two old ladies ran behind the counter where my uncle was. Richie R and I were behind the counter in the back of the store. When he ran in yelling "I want Richie!" I said to Richie R, "I think he wants you." Richie said, "No fucking way. He's looking for you!" At that, I ripped off my apron, grabbed a meat clever, and ran out from behind the counter and across the store. The PR turned and started to run out of the store. He had the machete in his right hand, and as he ran out the door, he hit my uncle's big picture window, now on his right. My uncle was yelling "No! No!" and the two old ladies were screaming as the whole window came down. I said to myself, "Now I'm fucked. I'm going to kill this motherfucker." As I ran out the door, two cops came running out of Benny's Luncheonette, diagonally across the street, with their guns out. They yelled at him to stop. He did and threw down the machete, yelling all the while, "Look what this guinea motherfucker did to me." He did look pretty bad. I told the cops, "I'm working in my uncle's butcher shop. I don't know what the fuck he's talking about." They put him in handcuffs, stuck him in the back of the cop car, and left. I never heard a thing about it again. My uncle was pissed, and I denied the whole thing; anyway, he had insurance. All these for two pairs of dungarees! As a young man, I tested it, always challenging and pushed. So I will just rejoice over the victory. Desperate times give the need for desperate remedies.

New Lots Boys versus the Unholy Alliance

It was the winter of 1960. East New York was rich in harmony and a closeness that cannot be found today. Today, people are ready to accept any kind of condition in order to win.

I was fifteen years old. I had been a New Lots Boy for two years. New Lots Avenue was the center of my world. My friends were my brothers by virtue of our many street crusades. It was one of those bone-chilling, cold nights. I got home from work at 6:30 p.m. I never missed a workout during the week, and it was Wednesday, but I couldn't get the chill out of me, so I took a hot shower and just let the hot water run on me until the chill was gone. I got dressed in a pair of jeans, a white T-shirt, a blue sweatshirt with a hood, a three-quarter-long black leather jacket, a pair of black skin gloves, and a pair of black gum sole desert boots, my personal fight gear. My mother asked, "Aren't you going to eat?" I said, "I'm going for a run. I'll eat when I come back." She said, "Don't go! I have a bad feeling!" Her bad feelings were usually right. When something happened to me or my brother and she had called it before it happened, we would call her a witch.

It was so cold out that it was too cold to snow. I thought I would run to New Lots Avenue and see if any of the guys were around. I was running north on Elton Street. When I got to Elton Street Park, just before New Lots Avenue, I looked in the park and there were the guys and the New Lots girls. My girlfriend at that time was Marietta, a cute Italian girl. I was always struck by the beauty of her face, not a single blemish. She had dark hair and dark brown eyes. She was shivering as I walked up to her and kissed her and held her trembling hands. I told her to go home and that I'd call her later that night. Our relationship didn't last very long. You see, mostly all of the girls from New Lots Avenue were sisters, cousins, or daughters of a New Lots boy. Marietta was the sister of one my friends, Tommy, and I had to respect the friendship. Some guys would never leave the corner; every day, you could count on seeing the same faces. A lot of those guys married New Lots girls. And then there were guys like me who would make friends and explore other neighborhoods for their fine young ladies.

Everyone was just hanging out in the cold, freezing their asses off. I was like, "I'm not hanging out in this shit. Does anyone want to go for a run?" There were about twelve guys there at that time; eight of them said, "Let's go!" The other four told me to go fuck myself; they weren't moving. We ran out the Linwood Street side of the park, ran south on Linwood to Hegeman Avenue, made a right heading west to Ashford Street, and made another right north heading to New Lots Avenue. As we got halfway up the block, we saw a large group of guys who we didn't recognize, standing in the cold dark street, so we slowed down to a walk. As we got closer, we could see that the gas station across the street from the East New York Boy's Club was full of Puerto Ricans and bros. Whenever the Spanish gangs hooked up with bros, it was out of desperation and it formed an unholy alliance. My experience on the street had taught me that unless the bros had big numbers and outnumbered you, they wouldn't stick; they'd even leave their people behind. The PRs knew this by now. They would stick; they were more like family.

We got up to the club and walked inside. As we were walking in, six Puerto Rican dudes were walking out. We looked at one another with cold contempt. These were bad-looking gang bangers, with bald heads, bandanas, and sweatshirts with hoods over their heads. This one big dude was wearing a pair of blue jeans and motorcycle boots and a leather vest with no shirt. He had huge arms; this dude was the first person I have ever seen that was covered with tattoos with no color. I found out later that they were called jailhouse tattoos. This is one bad-looking dude; mind you, it was subzero outside, and this guy has no shirt on. There were only a few of our guys in the boy's club. I said, "What the fuck is going on? There are a hundred fuckin' guys out there!" When a large deep voice echoed in the entrance of the club and said, "Not one of you guinea motherfuckers are coming out alive." I said, "There's a fat fuckin' chance of that, you fat piece of shit!" I ran outside and in the middle of the street was this big fat fuck. He had a hood on, and I couldn't see his face. He was wearing a full-length tan rain coat that was open, and he was holding a baseball bat in his right hand. The few of our guys that were in the boy's club followed me out; this dude was still yelling and calling us guinea motherfuckers. Now more of our guys were showing up from the park, Chester's and the Triangle luncheonettes on New Lots Avenue, and Frank's Bar, New Lots Boys hangouts. I ran out and straight at him. He looked a lot larger than he did in the club. It never crossed my mind that this fat fuck would be fast enough to tag me with that bat. When I got close up to him, I tried to get in by bobbing and weaving. The next thing I remembered was waking up in the middle of the gas station across the street. It wasn't the first and far from the last lesson I learned the hard way. I guess that fat fuck was a lot faster than I thought.

I could feel blood pouring from my nose and lips. My eyes opened slowly with a sidelong glance. In a flash, I could see this fat fuckin' Puerto Rican with his thick neck and a dark deep scarred face. He was sitting on my chest, striking me with lefts and rights. I have always believed that by striking me, he cleared the cobwebs from my brain. As soon as my head cleared a little, I quickly grabbed him by his face, pulling him down to me, and bit him on his face. Holding him with my left and banging him with short right hands, I tried to rip him off me by reaching around with my left hand and grabbing his mouth. He bit my fingers, ripping off two fingernails. I just remember him being so heavy. I was gasping for breath. I was spent. I felt myself going. I could sense there was an all-out war raging around me. The next thing I knew he was off me; my friend Sonny had kicked him in the face. Sonny was a true New Lots Boys, naturally strong and will hurt you. Before I could get up, this big fuck grabs me and throws me like I was a rag doll. While I was getting up, I had picked up a glass soda bottle, so at least I had a weapon in my hand as I went down for the second time. He's now on top of me again. I was still holding him close to me with my left hand so he couldn't get up to inflict more damage. I pulled him tighter to me now and cracked the bottle on the pavement with my right hand. I stuck him in the head, face, and neck with the jagged broken edges of the bottle. He was trying to get off me desperately. His blood was blinding me. Finally, I felt his body go limp. He was done. I rolled him off me.

I was finished. I heard the cops coming and everyone split. I was so finished that I was hardly able to get up. I walked home and almost didn't make it. When I did get home, my father was playing cards with his friends in the kitchen. My mother was washing dishes, and my brother was watching TV in the living room. The house I lived in was a two-family home on Elton Street two blocks south of Linden Boulevard; you entered into a small foyer. We lived on the first floor. The foyer door opened up into the living room, where my brother Frankie was watching TV in his typical TV gear, a T-shirt and a pair of boxer shorts. I walked past him without incident. My brother was four years older than I was and would always look at me like I had brain damage for fighting all the time. I had to make it past the kitchen without my dad or his friends or my mother seeing me. Fat chance! I looked like someone who had just gotten hit by a bus. So as I tried to breeze through the kitchen to get to the bathroom, I knew my father and his friends wouldn't look up from their card game, but my mother was another story; she had that built-in radar. I was halfway through the kitchen when she turned, looked at me, and yelled "What happened to you?" I was a mess; I had two black eyes, my nose was fractured, I had a chipped tooth, my lips were torn up, black and blue, and swollen, my skin was hanging from inside of my mouth, and two of my fingernails were torn half off. I walked straight to the bathroom. I could hardly stand up. I held onto the sink and put my head under the cold water.

My dad was a really nice guy. I never heard him say a negative thing about anyone. I never saw him nasty or mean. He loved the action of a good card or dice game and the ponies. If you interrupted a dice game or card game, it could get ugly. My dad and his friends jumped up when they heard my mother scream, and they all ran into the bathroom after me to find out what had happened. My father took a look at me and raised his hand to hit me; he was so mad. My father never hit me or my brother. When I picked up my head and he took one look at my face, I said, "If you can find a spot on my face, go for it." He put his hand down and said, "Don't you know how to run?"

Most of my education came from the streets of East New York, and by the ripe old age of fifteen years, I had a PhD in paralyzing stupidity, so the most intelligent thing I could say through swollen lips was "I don't run!" With that, the next thing I heard him say was "Are you a moron?" My father said, "It doesn't look like you won." I said, "I think I did." He said, "If I were you, I wouldn't rejoice in this victory." I don't even remember going to bed.

When I woke up in the morning, my two fingers that had been bitten were swollen and beating like crazy, so my dad took me to Doctor Meyerhof. He gave me a shot and told me a human bite was worse than a rat bite. Good, just what I needed to hear! The only satisfaction I got was that I knew that the big guy had to be in worse shape than I was.

I was still in high school at that time, at East New York Vocational High School. I had to take off from school, and with my friends coming over to see me every day, my father thought it might be a good idea to get me out of town and away from New Lots for a while.

He sent me to my grandparent's house. They lived in Deer Park, Long Island, New York, where they had a few small farms with chickens and goats. Every year, I would go out to Long Island and help Grandpa turn the dirt to plant for the season. My father knew his dad would keep me busy and out of trouble for a while. We fixed the chicken coop, built a few new fences, and worked on the house. We worked on my grandfather's wine cellar, with its dirt floor, stone walls, and ceiling. I loved it! He was a great, an honest man; he was quiet and with a good soul. My grandmother was a big woman who did not speak English. She would call us in for dinner, and that would be the highlight of my day. My grandmother made the best homemade macaroni and the best meat sauce I ever had; as I'm writing this, my mouth is watering. By the end of the week, my face was healing and my hands were full of blisters, with dirt under my fingernails, but I loved every minute.

Years later, when my grandfather died of cancer, the only things he had in his wallet were a hundred dollar bill and my army picture. My aunts gave me the hundred dollar bill as a gift, but the greatest gift was the time I spent with him.

That street war created a positive experience for me with my grandfather which I never would have had otherwise. Sometimes, the greatest bonds between people come about as a result of their experiences together.

Are the wars halfway around the world right and my wars in East New York wrong, or are all wars a necessary evil?

The Revenge of Richie Q versus the Unholy Alliance

The winter of 1960, I was beat up real bad outside the East New York Boy's Club. My dad sent me to work in Long Island with my grandfather on his farm to keep me away from the New Lots Boys. The story I'm about to tell you was told to me by Hi Ho.

Hi Ho was eighteen and doing six months extra in high school due to bad behavior. What a shock. A New Lots Boy engaged in bad behavior. Hi Ho said that someone in school ask him if he was involved in the fight on New Lots Avenue the previous night. Hi Ho said no and that he was home last night and didn't know anything about it. He found out that dozens of blacks and Puerto Rican came down to the boy's club where we hung out.

The East New York Club was part of the Boy's Clubs of America, a very worthy organization except for the fact that we hung out there. Our friend's father known as Bingo ran the place. Anybody could join, but when they looked in and saw the crew that hung out there, they said "no thanks." The PRs and the bros were armed with the usual East New York arsenal of bats, pipers, knives, car antennas, and whatever else could kill or maim a fellow human being. Inside, Bingo and a few of the New Lots Boys were there. They were taken by complete surprise. After threatening our guys inside to come outside, I came in with eight of our crew. We went for a run to stay warm on this frigate night. I was beat up real bad and barely made it home. After hearing the story in school, Hi Ho made sure he went to the boy's club the next night. When Hi Ho got to the club and walked inside, there he said were about seventy New Lots Boys plus Johnny Reb and his Rebels. Everyone is armed to the teeth.

I was home nursing my wounds, so Hi Ho and our crew went that night to avenge my getting fucked up. The word on the street was that the PRs and bros want to meet the New Lots Boys on Blake Avenue and Ashford Street. Usually, these prearranged fights never take place. Hi Ho told me to his surprise when they got to Blake Avenue, they were greeted by what looked like an entire army division. There was at least a couple of hundred armed Puerto Rican and black warriors. The El Tones had the help from the Roman Lords.

Hi Ho said as he walked up to them, he was carrying the handle of a sanitation shovel with iron sides. Standing next to him was Pokie, who was carrying a sawed off 22 rifle in his coat. Hi Ho told me he couldn't wait to see what was going to happen when he pulls out the rifle. Our guys also thought that the PRs may come with guns. Our guys walked up to them, and there's this big bro standing on a stoop. He asked if we were the New Lots Boys; we said, "Ya and who the fuck are you?" He offered to fight anyone of us. There were a few hundred guys armed to the teeth, and this dude was looking for a fair fight. This guy wants an option. Ira said, "We are not here to fuck one of you up. We are here to fuck all of you up."

Pokie walked up, took the rifle out from under his coat, and pointed it at the dude on the steps. Hi Ho said you could see the terror in this guy's eyes. To make matters worse, Pokie was shaking, and it looked like the gun might go off. This guy was begging Pokie to point the gun away from him. Hi Ho was getting bored and told Pokie to shoot this motherfucker. Bang! The gun went off, and the bro went flying of the stoop, then our guys started kicking ass. No one knew till the next night that when Hi Ho told Pokie to shoot, Richie S walked up to the guy on the stoop and hit him with a straight right hand. This dude went down as the gun went off. No one saw Richie hit this guy; all they heard was the shot. The New Lots crew destroyed the El Tones and the Roman Lords; half had run when the gun went off. When our crew got back to New Lots Avenue, everyone still thought Pokie had shot the guy. One of our friends told Hi Ho that if Pokie killed this guy, he was just as guilty as Pokie was. Hi Ho said he hadn't thought about that at all. Of course, everybody on both sides heard him yell it out. He told our friend Ronnie to drive him to Canarsie. He thought he would get some guys that he knew there to say he was hanging with them at the time of the shooting what an alibi. This crew had its share of misfits and lunatics. Hi Ho had told them what happen, and they all agreed to say he was with them all night. Hi Ho was grasping for straws.

Hi Ho had an uneasy feeling all night. The next day in school, everybody was talking about the incident the night before. No one knew if the guy that got shot died. There was no word about the incident in any of the New York newspapers. Hi Ho said he was scared as shit and could picture him and Pokie side by side in twin electric chairs saying good-bye to each other. Hi Ho went to the boy's club that night. When he walked in, everybody was talking about what a great time they had and it would be a long time before the El Tones came back to New Lots Avenue. When Richie S walked in and said, "How do you guys like that I hit that dude standing on the steps? I knocked out that tough guy with one punch." No one knew what he was talking about. Then he explained what had happened. Hi Ho said when Richie told him what happened, he felt great. His nightmare was over, and no more murder rap hanging over him. Pokie was furious; he was so disappointed that he didn't shoot the guy.

It was a long time before the El Tones came back to New Lots Avenue. When they did come back, one of the El Tones a guy named Chino shot Jimmy Garcia, a PR that hung with us, in the head. He didn't die but was badly hurt. Sonny and his father Bingo grabbed the guy and almost beat him to death.

Another time, the El Tones were caught by the cops on their way to New Lots Avenue. One of them had a loaded shotgun. When the cops asked him where he was going with it, he said he was looking for New Lots Boys to shoot. In the meantime, the El Tones got many more beatings from the New Lots Boys.

Jimmy Garcia died ten years after being shot in the head. The story was that he should have had a plate in his head but the doctors never put one in. To the guy that Richie knocked out, he saved your life. I'm sure your jaw is OK but your heart wouldn't be if Pokies' bullet had hit its target as was his intention. As for the revenge of Richie Q, Hi Ho said the violent night on Blake Avenue was a good time had by one and all, if you were a New Lots Boys.

New Lots Boys versus Puerto Rican Turf: Round 1

In the early 1960s, Sutter Avenue became pretty much a stronghold for the Puerto Rican gangs. So in order to get anywhere north of Sutter Avenue, for any white teenager at that time, you would be pretty much taking your life in your own hands. It was a Saturday night, one of the hottest days of the summer yet, with high humidity and temperatures in the triple digits. A bunch of us were hanging out at the Triangle, bored and sweating. We needed somewhere to go with air conditioning. I heard about a dance at the Americana Bowling Alley, which was in Ozone Park, in Queens, New York. Now, mind you, most of us weren't very good dancers, but I heard there were a lot of cute girls there. I told the guys about the dance, and eleven of us decided to go.

We decided to take the bus, which happened to be on Sutter Avenue. We had to walk from the Triangle, from Ashford Street and New Lots Avenue, about three-quarters of a mile to the corner of Shepherd and Sutter Avenues; not a good move on our part, but we were New Lots Boys, and just a few years ago, we could have walked anywhere in East New York and felt safe. But not anymore; those days went out together with the DA hairstyle. Consciously, we knew there would be thorns in our path.

I think I knew at that time that walking to Sutter Avenue was a deliberate act, subconsciously knowing we would never get to the bowling alley. It was amazing, but we did make it to the bus stop without a problem. As we were waiting for the bus, some Spanish guys were gathering in the street. More than likely, they were El Tones and Larkey Stompers from the Cypress Hills Housing Project; that was their turf. There were about twenty-five guys in the street, and more were coming. We had our backs against a four-foot iron fence. Behind the fence was a two-story brick house. Our backs were literally against the wall. We had nowhere to go.

This was it, and you knew if you were up against that many Puerto Ricans, some of us were bound to get stabbed. We had some pretty stand-up guys with us: Big Dave, Bruno, Jerry, Arnie, the Mick, Charlie Red, Charlie Jones, Sonny, Flash, and me, the Q. The next thing I knew, the Mick yelled, "New Lots!" and ran into the street. They rushed him; he backed up, hit the curb, and fell back onto the sidewalk. When I saw the Mick go down, that was it for me. I ran into the street throwing punches and growling; I always had that growl. The Mick told me later that when he went down, the only thing he heard was my growl and that he felt covered. Everyone simultaneously went to war. We were kicking ass! One guy threw a bat at me; it just missed my head. I ran to pick it up and when I did, I saw it had a spike running through its head. As that same guy ran past me, I yelled to Arnie to grab that motherfucker. Arnie grabbed him and so did Charlie Red. I ran up to him and grabbed him by the hair. By this time, there were dozens of guys in the street. We backed off and regrouped. I still had this guy by the hair, holding him with my left hand and had the bat in my right hand. As we kept backing off, I told the PRs that if they took one more step, I'd crack that motherfucker's head.

With all those guys, they still didn't have the balls to rush us. I was in the middle of the street holding that guy by the hair and backing up when they started to rush us. So I cracked him twice in his fucking head with the spike. After seeing that, they stopped for a minute. Arnie and I picked him up and threw him through a store window, directly across the street from the bus stop. At that point, everything stopped! They backed off again, and we split back to New Lots Avenue. They tried to give a half-assed chase. I brought up the rear with Big Davey, who was having a hard time keeping up.

We were tired and out of breath, and they didn't seem to be too eager to catch us. I still had the bat. For as bad as it could have been for us, I can't remember anyone of us getting damaged. I couldn't stop thinking that just a few years ago, life was so different. East New York in the early days seemed to me just a sea of good will. From as early as I can remember, I was playing street games with my friends Anthony D, Louie P, and Frankie G and dreaming of my first love, Lillian S, the cutest little blond who moved to Ozone Park, Queens, and broke my heart when I was ten years old. All I knew was at that time of my life, I wanted to work and have my own money. I shined shoes, collected soda bottles for their deposit money of two cents a bottle, and delivered circulars for the Speedway Supermarket. They paid three dollars to deliver one hundred circulars. Most of the guys would throw half of them down the sewers, but I would deliver every single one; it was better than feeling guilty for the rest of the night.

My first real job was working in my Uncle Frank's butcher shop on New Lots Avenue and Elton Street. As the delivery boy. I was twelve years old, and I had a bike with the large basket on the front. I would deliver all over East New York, parts of Brownsville, Canaries, and Queens. I was paid a large sum of ten dollars a week plus tips, and I was happy to have a job. I always had honest money in my pocket. (The New York City political system believed they needed to control the new social movement that was rapidly devolving in parts of the city with lower income, where people felt the intrusion and frustration.) I believed in hard work and all its benefits. But there were strangers among us with unfamiliar personality patterns. (Power always thinks it has a great soul and vast views. Consider what calamities that engine of grief has produced.)

New Lots Boys versus the Old Mill

It was 1960. Bobby Chink, Jimmy D, and I were hanging out in front of Izzy's candy store on Atkins and Hegeman Avenue, across the street from PS 202. I remember it being a clear summer's day. I was always working, so I'm not sure why I was off that day. I had just had an egg cream, and I went outside to talk to Jimmy and Chink. We hung out on the corner for a while. I said, "Why don't we go to the park or the Triangle and hook up with some of our guys and maybe start a punchball game?"

We walked west on Hegeman Avenue. I had a day off, and I wasn't going to let it go to waste. We walked two blocks to Shepherd Avenue. A block away, there were three guys walking toward us. As they got closer, I recognized one of the guys—G-Man, a guy I knew from Crescent Street. He was a tough guy with a reputation for being out of his mind, another one of those crazy characters raised in East New York's troubled environment. Once I saw G-Man and his cousin John throwing stolen bowling balls from Stanly Avenue north up Crescent Street across Linden Boulevard, a six-lane major road through East New York; they were missing cars, hitting cars, and causing accidents. These two lost their way years ago.

John married my cousin Marie, who also was a lost species of the same environment. John was an Italian, about five feet eight with a stocky build. He once had a shootout with his neighbor, who was a female with a bad attitude. No one got shot, and so the woman thought it was over and went to work that day. John owned a carting business and had heavy equipment; he took one of his bulldozers and cleared the angry white woman's property, including the house. A few years later, he contracted AIDS from a black prostitute. While he was in the hospital, my cousin Marie went to visit him. By that time, he was in very bad shape; he needed an oxygen tank to breathe.

When Marie walked into the room, he wanted to know if she would take care of him when he came home. She said, "Oh! You need someone to take care of you?" and walked out the door. A few seconds later, she walked back into the room with the prostitute. The girl's hands were tied and she was beaten up. Marie tossed the girl on to the bed and told John, "Here ya go! She took care of you before; she can take care of you again." John was released from the hospital, and a short time after that, they found the prostitute shot dead. After a while, John died of AIDS.

G-Man was just as crazy. He was a paid arsonist for people who needed insurance claims. Both those two sick fucks, it seemed to me, specialized in demonic worship. The day I met G-Man, I was hanging out in Elton Street Park with my friends. It was a nice, peaceful Sunday afternoon. G-Man and two of his friends were passing by the park. I was on the Linwood Street side of the park with a few of my friends. Frank Bep and a couple of our guys were on the Elton Street side of the park. G-Man and a couple of guys were passing south on the Elton Street side. As they passed the entrance of the park, G-man said something to Frankie Bep. Frankie gave the New Lots whistle for the New Lots Boys, and we came running. When G-Man and his crew saw us, they began running south on Elton Street then made a left on Hegeman Avenue and a right onto Linwood Street to Linden Boulevard, a six-lane road. I caught up to G-Man in the middle of Linden Boulevard, and as he was still running, I cracked him in the back of the head with a right hand. He went forward and down. Cars were coming at us from both directions. I picked him up by his jacket, and we ran to the other side of Linden Boulevard. Frankie and the guys grabbed this guy Joey D. Our guys were cool with Joey; they never touched him. All G-Man could say was "Where did all you fucking guys come from?" Frankie Bep said, "This is New Lots, motherfucker!" We talked for a while, and they told us they were from Crescent Street and the old mill. The old mill was off Crescent Street, south of Linden Boulevard, and most of the young men in the area had the same demonic traits. We kind of became good friends that day. Don't ask me why, but I liked the guy's character. Teens in those early 1960s had to run the gauntlet and maneuver the mean streets of East New York.

I still continued to work out hard and was growing in skills. As G-Man and his two friends got closer to us, I could see one of G-Man's friends was posturing, like he was one bad ass dude. I said, "Look at this guy!" Chink said, "I know this prick. He ain't shit. I once kicked his ass." Bobby Chink, named Chink because he wore those thick, coke-bottle glasses, he was about five feet four and blind as a bat. G-Man and the other two guys walked up to us. I shook his hand and introduced Jimmy and Chink, and G-Man did the same. I asked G-Man and his friends if they wanted to come to the park and told them that we were looking to start a punchball game. G-Man said, "We can't; my friend has to go to karate school. He has a black belt and is in an exhibition tonight." I said, "How cool is that!" This guy was the first karate guy I had ever met, and he was no less than a black belt. Chink looked at this dude and said, "What are you talking about? I kicked this punk's ass last year!" The guy looked at Chink and said, "I've never even met this four-eyed fucking midget." Now don't forget, Chink was as blind as a bat, and that dude didn't look like a slouch. Karate was becoming a big thing, and I had heard stories about how bad karate guys were; and to be in the Army Special Forces, you had to know karate. I was thinking to myself, "Fucking Chink's libel to get my ass and Jimmy's ass kicked along with his."

There was a vacant lot on Sheppard Avenue and Linden Boulevard, a block away from where we were, so I said, "Why don't we go to the empty lot down the block and you two can get it on?" He turned and looked at me and said, "After I knock out the midget, you're next!" I was thinking, "OK. This guy just might kick my ass, with all that shit he's talking, but while he's trying, he will get damaged." So the dude said, "Let's do it, motherfuckers." I was not liking this guy, but I had to see what he had and at Chink's expense by the looks of it. When we got halfway down the block, I told Chink, "You fuck him up now." The dude was walking in front of us. G-Man and the other guy didn't say a word. Chink took off his glasses and handed them to Jimmy. Then Chink ran up and jumped on the dude's back. The guy flipped Chink over his shoulder and cracked him with two beautiful straight right hands, knocking him out. Chink was lying on the sidewalk, like he was sleeping on a park bench. It happened so fast that we all just looked at one another, like "What the fuck just happened?" I was now thinking, "This guy is good and quick." The next move the dude, or now Mr. Dude, made touched my nerve; he bent down at the waist, making hand motions like he was dusting off his pants at the same time saying, "I didn't want to hurt the midget."

The next time I saw G-Man, he told me that he knew as soon as his friend said he didn't want to hurt the midget what was about to go down. As this dude bent down, I threw a right kick to his face. As his head came up, I right handed him twice, moving forward. I knocked him out! Next to us was an apartment building. About three feet from the building, there was a four-foot iron fence. When I hit that guy with the second shot, the dude spun and fell with his face over the fence. I thought for a few seconds that maybe he was dead; he didn't move. G-Man and the other guy ran into the street. I just said, "Pick up your friend and never come to New Lots with a scumbag like this again." G-Man and I stayed pretty good friends. We never got to play punchball that day. G-Man continued to do some sick fucking things, until he fucked with some wise guy's wife and caught a bullet. There are some things you just don't do. Chink could hardly stand up. I said, "You sure taught him a thing or two about a thing or two." We went to the corner across from the Triangle on Livonia Avenue, where there was the terminal luncheonette. I had a vanilla malt and a piece of apple pie. There was no way you grew up in East New York without knowing someone who became a wise guy; was killed, raped, mugged, went to jail, became a junkie or a dealer. Talk about a great awakening!

NEW LOTS BOYS VERSUS EL TONES AND EL QUINTOS

It was the winter of 1961. I quit school. Looking back, I realize that I had contempt for the way the educators during those times made me feel. I love to physically work. I landed a great job working in the carpet business, five days a week, as a helper for Consumer Carpets. I didn't work on Saturdays, so I would work at my Uncle Frank's butcher shop. Once in a while, when I didn't have work during the week for Consumer Carpets, I would work at the butcher shop for my uncle.

It was Thursday. I didn't have work at Consumer Carpets, so I went to the butcher shop to work. Thursday was a pretty slow day. At noon, Mr. Nero, the park man at Elton Street Park, came to the butcher shop and asked me if I could get away for lunch. No one was in the shop, and all my work was basically done, so I told Mr. Nero, "Let's go, and this time I'll pay." Most of the time, he wouldn't let me go into my pocket. When we had the time, we would go across the street from the butcher shop to Benny's Luncheonette on New Lots Avenue for the best tuna, lettuce, and tomato on toast and a piece of coconut custard pie for desert. We would wash it down with Dr. Brown's Cel-Ray Soda, which was the best! I believe the friendship we had was a mutual respect for each other; even though I was so much younger than Mr. Nero, he would speak to me as his equal.

My parents gave me my values, and Mr. Nero gave me my style and character. Every time I would be in a difficult situation, I would ask myself what would Mr. Nero do. When I was introduced to him by the guys, they had introduced him to me as Mr. Nero. I was thirteen years old then, and Mr. Nero was mid to late thirties. He was a small guy, about five feet six, with a bald head, and he was in great shape. He was a black man that everyone in

---

the neighborhood respected. When I first met him, he was giving Anthony Stabile boxing lessons in the park house.

I would run to the park house every day after school, and Mr. Nero would be waiting to give me lessons for half an hour before I had to go to work. I always thought of him as my mentor and considered myself fortunate to know the man. At that time, I didn't realize what an impact he would have on my life. We remained good friends for many years, and that friendship could be a book all by itself. We had lunch and some good laughs, and I went back to work. I bought my uncle a container of coffee, and I bought myself a container of hot chocolate. It was cloudy and very cold. You could smell snow in the air. I looked at my uncle in his large ill-fitted starched white butcher coat. I said, "It's pretty slow today." He said, "Who the hell would come out in this weather?" The front of the store had a big picture window. There wasn't much to do, so I took my hot chocolate and leaned against the counter in front of the window and watched as people walked by freezing. It was pretty much a typical butcher shop of the times, with a wooden floor covered with sawdust that we would rake every evening.

We would lay new sawdust every Saturday night at closing. The two showcases were white porcelain. The ice box was in the back. We closed at six o'clock every evening, except Fridays, in which the shop closed at nine o'clock in the evening. It was now after three o'clock, and there wasn't much going on outside. Kids were coming home from school. While I was looking out the window, I saw six Puerto Ricans with bald heads and bandannas holding car antennas for weapons. They were chasing three high school kids coming home from Thomas Jefferson. They were running east on New Lots Avenue. They were now across the street from the butcher shop. As they passed, my uncle said, "Mind your own business." So I did! I ripped off my apron and ran out of the butcher shop. Here I was pursuing six savage-looking Puerto Rican guys. I was always prepared for war, and my uncle was right when he told me to mind my own business; New Lots was my business!

I didn't have much of a plan, or should I say I had no plans; what kind of plan could I have had? I was one white dude chasing six dudes with car antennas. Some people might think of it as having courage. I did things like this deliberately to deny my fears. I caught up to the last PR at Essex Street and New Lots Avenue, in front of Patsy's Barber Shop. Directly across the street was Saint Gabriel Rectory.

I grabbed the last guy and threw him against the barber shop window. I was throwing him a beating when his boys came back to help him, whipping me on my head and back. I didn't see the first guy, but I heard him say "Motherfucker!" As I turned, he caught me on my neck with the antenna. I felt the sting! He had the antenna in his right hand. I grabbed his right arm before he could get another shot. I straight right handed him a perfect shot to his throat, grabbed him, and threw him into the next two that were rushing me. The other two were right behind them. At that moment, my friend Ira, who happened to be getting a haircut in the barber shop, ran out to help. Also passing in a dump truck were Tommy P and Louie B. They jumped out of the truck, and Ira, Tommy, and Louie began to kick ass. The guy I hit in the throat was on the ground gasping for air. The five other guys couldn't get away fast enough. I chased one guy and caught him across the street, in front of the rectory where the nuns lived. I grabbed him and threw him down onto the rectory steps. He was a pretty big dude, so I didn't give him the opportunity to set himself. I held him down by his face and banged him with a barrage of right hands. Tommy and Louie came running to help. I told Tommy to hold his right arm and Louie to hold his left arm. I could see he was in a daze. I grabbed him by the hair. He was still able to look at me and say, "I'm going to come back with a shotgun." I told him, "You sorry piece of shit, it was going to have to be your brother 'cause you're dead."

As I began breaking up his face, the nuns came out of the rectory screaming. There was hysteria in their voices. I was in the blankness of the moment, but to the nuns, I am sure it was nightmarish and savage. Even Tommy grabbed me and said, "Q, he's had enough." As soon as Tommy grabbed me, I seemed to regain consciousness. I only had a T-shirt on, and I could feel the chill in the air go through me for the first time since I ran out of the butcher shop. I looked up at the nuns. There wasn't a thing I could say in my defense, and I didn't try. I just said sorry, and we split. Tommy and Louie ran back to their truck, Ira went back to getting his haircut, and I ran back to work.

I always remember things like this happening on New Lots Avenue. If anyone was in trouble, it just looked like guys would pop out of nowhere. When I got back to the shop, my uncle said, "When we get home, I'm going to tell your mother." My mother was his sister. I didn't hear another word he was saying. My adrenalin was still pumping. All I could see was the contempt on the faces of the nuns and what they were thinking. They had no knowledge of what had gone down; all they witnessed was my savage behavior and this bloody Puerto Rican guy lying on the pavement. In my own defense, we were outnumbered. We had no weapons, and it felt morally right. You, the reader, can judge for yourself. It may have been the way Puerto Ricans grew up in Puerto Rico. I never heard of them calling the cops. They were more like us in that the cops would get in the way.

What I knew was that there would be a ripple effect. They would be back in force, and we would have no idea when they were coming. We knew we would have to be prepared for war.

NEW LOTS BOYS VERSUS BROWNSVILLE PRs: THE RIPPLE EFFECT

It was 1961. We did prepare for war! We knew this would be a big one and that they would scout out New Lots and catch us short; that was the word on the street. On really cold nights, we hung out at the Triangle, at the East New York Boy's Club, or at someone's cellar, where the New Lots girls could hang with us. Not even a week had gone by, and we were hanging out in Frankie P's cellar, on the corner of Linwood Street and New Lots Avenue, when Mouse came running down the hallway steps yelling that there were hundreds of spics at the Triangle. There were only about ten of us in the cellar. We had bats and pipes hidden there, so we each grabbed a weapon and started to go up the cold concrete steps and out the two iron doors that opened on to the street. We were already hearing sirens in the streets. Arnie was the first guy to stick his head out of one of the iron doors when we heard a blast. Later on, we heard that it was a shotgun blasted at a cop car. Arnie pushed us back into the cellar. We ran up the cellar steps leading to the hallway. I looked out the front door, but there wasn't anything going on in front of us. I looked to my right and could see a load of cop car lights at the Triangle. I told the girls to go and wait downstairs. I told Mouse and the rest of the guys to stay put. There were too many cops on the avenue. I told Arnie to follow me. We walked across New Lots Avenue, south on Linwood Street, half a block to Elton Street Park. The park was between Elton and Linwood Streets. We went into the park. Ralph Boccio and Mike Berganti were in the park. As soon as they saw us come into the park, they ran to us from the Elton Street side and asked, "What the fuck is happening on the avenue?

It's filled with cop cars, and we heard some gunshots." I said, "The El Tones and the El Quintos came to the corner looking for us." The El Tones were a Puerto Rican gang out of East New York. Most of the El Quintos came out of Brownsville. I asked Mike Berganti if he had his car, and he said yes. I said, "Go get it and meet me on Hegeman Avenue under the elevator." I ran south on the Linwood Street side of the park. Arnie followed me, and Ralph went with Mike. I ran through a hole in the park fence under the elevator, the EL, where they housed the IRT trains.

The old neighborhood Italian guys, like my grandfather, would play boccie ball on the weekends under the EL. The EL was held up by large, tall metal columns. A couple of weeks earlier, Foxie and I had made six gas bombs and put them in two shopping bags, with two Zippo lighters, and we'd stuffed them into one of the columns. I could see Mike and Ralph were just turning the corner on Linwood Street and Hegeman Avenue. I ran to the column where I had put the bags and pulled out four gas bombs and two lighters. I gave two bombs and a Zippo to Arnie, and I grabbed two bombs and a Zippo. Gas bombs were made out of glass soda bottle filled with gas and a rag wet with gas, six inches inside the bottle and six inches out of the bottle. Arnie and I ran to Mike Berganti's car. I asked Mike to drive past the Triangle. There were still cops all over the avenue, but no PRs, so we drove west, up New Lots Avenue. When we got to the Biltmore Theater, which is about three-quarters of a mile from the Triangle, there they were, just hanging out in front of the theater. The theater was on New Lots Avenue, just off the corner of Miller Avenue. I told Mike to make a right turn just before we got to Miller Avenue. He made the right turn, drove to the next block, which was Riverdale Avenue, then made a left to Miller Avenue. I told Mike to double park and wait there with Ralph. Arnie and I got out of the car with our gas bombs and walked south on Miller Avenue. There were at least fifty guys on the corner. The corner was packed with a few bros and mostly Puerto Ricans. If these guys were this far up New Lots Avenue, they were most likely headed back to Brownsville, the community west of East New York. This told me that with these many guys, the El Tones had to be hooked up with other gangs out of East New York, gangs like the El Quintos, the Roman Lords, or the Bishops, or maybe even the Chaplains, the largest black gang in Brooklyn. It was cold. We were wearing black three-quarter length leather jackets with two deep straight side pockets; each pocket held one gas bomb. I had on black chino pants, gum sole shoes, and skin gloves. Arnie had the worst hygiene; his leather jacket was filthy and torn; his blue jeans were the same, and his shoes were regular leather shoes that were too large, with holes and no laces and an overpowering smell of sweat. But the dude could run twice as fast as I could with those shoes on, go figure.

We got about twenty feet away from where all those dudes were hanging. In a few seconds, before we had to make our move, I took the gas bomb out of my right pocket and had the lighter in my left hand. Arnie did the same. There were leather flaps on the jacket, concealing and protecting the other bottle. We were still walking closer, and Arnie smiled this boyish smile, telling me he was ready. I yelled, "Mira, motherfucker!" They all turned and looked in our direction. We stopped about fifteen feet away. Without looking at each other, we lit up at the same time and yelled "New Lots!" The first bombs hit the pavement in front of them and a telephone pole, a couple of feet to their right. We pulled out the other two bottles from our left pockets, even before the first two landed, never taking our eyes off our target. They landed in the street; there were no real targets. After the first bombs hit, there was fire all over. Guys were running in every direction; the whole street was in commotion. We began to run backward so we could watch where the bombs had landed, and then we turned and ran back to Mike Berganti's car. As we were running back, Arnie said, "Hey, Q! I'm starving!" He had no job and knew I worked two jobs and always had money. When we got back to the car, Ralph said, "From here, it looked like you motherfuckers lit up all of New Lots Avenue." Arnie said, "We did!" Mike said, "Where to now?" I said, "Fulton and Cleveland Streets." Mike Berganti said, "Where?" "Fulton and Cleveland, Moe's Bar!" Moe made the best chicken parmesan heroes, and it was out of our area of East New York. (Being a New Lots Boy made me feel proud. I was part of something larger than myself. In my case, passion disputes the laws.)

NEW LOTS BOYS VERSUS CYPRESS HILLS BROS

In the spring of 1961, the Cypress Hills Housing Project was the worst housing development in East New York, from Fountain Avenue, west of Euclid Avenue, east of Sutter Avenue north, and south of Linden Boulevard. The projects were a breeding ground for crime, dominated by mostly black gangs. Killings, burglaries, drugs, cowardly muggings of woman and seniors, discarding unwanted newborn babies, and mutilations of dogs and cats were weekly in the daily news. The elevators, halls, and steps smelled of urine. Life was hard enough for the poor honest hardworking people trying to better themselves with mostly low-paying jobs and dreams of moving their family to a little home in Queens with their own small patch of Kentucky blue grass where their children could grow up and go to school without the threat of violent encounters. Where they could have a sense of freedom and safety, where human values exist. The ugly fact is there was a cry for help, and I have no other words or way to say this. The scumbag New York City political system that created this mess was now deaf.

Big Davy lived in the Cypress Hills Housing Project, a seven-story building on the southeast corner of Linden Boulevard and Fountain Avenue. It was hard enough being a young teenage white boy living in the project. To make matters worse for Davy, he was a New Lots Boy. Most of the kids from the project went to PS 202 grade school, so we were pretty familiar with the bros that lived and hung out with the gangs in Cypress Hills. One day, Big Davy had to catch a bus on the corner of Linden Boulevard and Fountain Avenue to take a night class when he was approached by this hard-faced bulky-looking bro and his crew. Big Davy was fifteen years old. By this time in Big Davy's life, he knew and could smell the threat. Davy was a banger, and as the dude got within his punching space, Big Davy hit this dude with a straight right hand. The last thing Davy remembered was getting hit in the back of the head with a hard object and waking up on the sidewalk with a headache and a cut on his upper lip. He went back to his apartment, and his mother went with him to the hospital where he received a few stitches on his upper lip. When he got back home that night, he called me at my house and told me what had happened. He said he knew most of the bros that had approached him and they went to PS 64 Junior High School. That night, I called a few of our guys, Foxy—Ronald Jerothe, Arnie, Sonny, and Big Louie P, and told them to meet me at the Triangle tomorrow at two o'clock. It was about a half an hour to a forty-minute walk to PS 64 from the Triangle. We got to the school about 2:45 p.m.

PS 64 was south of Belmont Avenue and had exits on the east side of the school. Berriman Street and the west side entry were on Atkins Avenue. We had heard that most of the bros came out on the Atkins Avenue side. Across the street from the school were two attached family brick homes from north of Belmont Avenue. Halfway up the block, the rest of that side of the block was the schoolyard playground. There were about eight of us fighters, and all were dependable, which always gave us the edge. We also had the element of surprise. We leaned against and sat on the stoops of a couple of houses across the Atkins Avenue side school entrance. In a few minutes, these guys would be exiting. We knew we would have to hit hard and fast and inflict as much serious damage as possible before the cops came. I would have to say to our credit we had no weapons; that's how much confidence we had in our street-fighting abilities. At three o'clock on the dot, the school bell rang, and it was loud. Within seconds, the metal school doors flung open, and there was a mad rush to the street. It was sort of wild and to me a little confusing, until I saw a cute little blonde white girl being pulled outside by her hair by three black girls while the bros cheered them on, trying to get some feels. That was more than a good enough sign for me. We all rushed in, banging. The bros couldn't get away fast enough, tripping all over one another. We did a pretty good job of laying out a few in the middle of Atkins Avenue when we heard the cops coming. That was the sign, and we're really not looking to confront hostile police, so as we start to run north on Atkins Avenue, there was Big Louie P, walking. I yelled, "Yo, the cops are coming!" He shrugged and said, "So what? I didn't do anything." We kept running, got to Pitkin Avenue, turned right, and ran to Crescent Street north to Atlantic Avenue and the Lucky Strike Bowling alley, where we washed up and had a couple of sodas.

I called Davy from the Bowling alley and told him the good news. I also told him to watch his ass. We made our way back to the Triangle; Big Davy never had an incident in the project like that again. At about the same time, there was a young Puerto Rican guy from Cypress that hung with us. We called him Jivo. His brother hung with a PR gang called the Larkey Stompers. Jivo became a turncoat and tried to set up a few of our guys with his brother's crew. When Sonny found this out, he went to the project with a few of the guys and gave Jivo a beating in his own apartment. I figure these two incidents left a good message. If you're wondering what happened to Big Louie P, he was busted by the cops. To make matters worse, the cops busted a few white guys that hung out on the corner of Berriman and Belmont Avenues. They were all taken by paddy wagon to the Seventh-fifth Precinct on the corner of Liberty and Miller Avenues. These guys wanted to kill Louie. Most of the time, Big Louie P was pretty indifferent. That day was no exception; he was, like, fuck you.

Big Louie P was a big guy with a face shadow at a very young age, making him look more like a man. They all denied being in a fight, and Big Louie P naturally had no idea what the cops were talking about. They were let go, and as mad as the guys from Berriman and Belmont were, they know better than to fuck up a New Lots Boy. I heard a few of these guys from Berriman and Belmont were pretty bad guys but apparently not stupid. So our street crusades continued. This was a tough, cruel game. The powers that be had us in. I went back home that night, sat on my stoop, looked around, and found that just a couple of years ago, I played games on these streets on the stoops and down the alleyways. My mother came out and asked, "Why are you just sitting here? Come in. I'll make you something to eat." I was thinking that this is bad, and I knew it was about to get worse. To me, it had its fascination.

THE NEW LOTS BOYS VERSUS HEMLOCK AND SUTTER

It was 1961. I was sixteen years old. I thought I had a sense of purpose, and that purpose was to have as many positive experiences as I could in my little world. It was a beautiful fall Friday night. I came home from work, took a shower, had dinner, and got dressed in my typical fight gear—comfortable slacks, a loose fitting shirt, and gum sole shoes.

Like every day, out of my dear mother's mouth came those words of encouragement, "Are you going to hang out with those bums from New Lots?" All I answered was "I love ya, Mom," and I was out the door, headed to New Lots. I was walking north on Elton Street, and as I passed Elton Street Park, some of my friends and a few of the older guys were hanging out. The park was divided in to two parts: the Linwood Street side and the Elton Street side. The IRT train line ran right through the center of the park, twenty feet above the ground on the way home to what was called "the barn."

I walked into the park up to the guys on the Linwood Street side and said, "What's going on?" They said, "Nothing! Where are you going?" I told them I had to meet Big Davy, Foxy, and a few of my guys on New Lots. I told them I had met a couple of girls at the St. Fortunata's dance the week before and they had invited me to a party. I had asked them if I could bring a couple of my friends, and they had said, "Yes, as many as you like."

The New Lots Boys had at that time five different age groups: the men, who were forty-five or so, who didn't leave the corner; the next group aged from twenty-one to thirty years; the next group aged from eighteen to twenty years; the guys I hung out with were aged sixteen and seventeen years; and the tots, who were aged twelve to fourteen years. By 1961, we were just starting to integrate, mostly the sixteen-to twenty-year-olds.

So I said, "Do you guys want to go to the party?" There was Hi Ho, Schmitty, and Sandy, who were two and three years older than me, and my friend Steve was hanging with them at that time. Hi Ho said, "We were just talking about what we were going to do tonight." I said, "There you go man!" Hi Ho said, "How are you guys getting there?" I said, "We're walking." Just then, Detective Finn drove up in his gray 1959 Buick.

Detective Finn worked in the First Precinct headquarters, Manhattan ballistics. Here was a guy, a detective, who just showed up one day and never gave us a reason. At that time, he was, I'd say, in his midthirties, about five feet nine and one hundred and fifty pounds. Whenever he came around, he would pick up some of the guys and drive them wherever they wanted to go. He'd take them to dinner and pick up the tab. It made no sense to me.

One day, he happened to just drive up to the Linwood Street side of the park. A few of us guys were playing punchball. Big Davy and Frankie B were there hanging out. They jumped into Finn's car, and the next thing we knew, Big Davy said Frankie pulled a gun out of Finn's glove compartment and pointed it at Finn's head. Finn pleaded with Frankie to put the gun down, and so did Big Davy; they knew that Frankie was out of his mind and just might have put a bullet in Finn's head. But Frankie gave Finn back his gun, and Finn never did anything about it; he still kept coming around.

Another time, Finn told Sandy and a few of the guys to take a ride with him to Queens. He stopped at a bar and told the guys to wait in the car. He said, "The guys in this bar are real bad guys." So our guys were waiting in Finn's car when out came a few guys from the bar, with Finn in tow. One guy leaned on the passenger side of Finn's car and stuck his face into the open window where Sandy was sitting. He looked right into Sandy's face and said, "Where are these punks from?" Before that dude had gotten the last word out, Sandy grabbed him with his left hand, pulled him inside the car, and cracked him with a solid right, knocking him back and down while saying, "New Lots, motherfucker!" The rest of his crew ran back into the bar. Stuff like this would happen day after day. We never figured out what Finn wanted from us; he appeared one day and a few months later disappeared. He was for real. We had seen him at the police headquarters in lower Manhattan and at the Seventh-Fifth Precinct on the corner of Liberty and Miller Avenues.

So the night of the party, there was Finn at the Linwood Street entrance of the park. Hi Ho said, "There's our ride!" We ran up to Finn's car and told him to take us to the corner. He asked, "Where are you going?" I said, "Hemlock and Sutter." When we got to the corner, Sonny, Big Davy, Foxy, Joey Jet, Ross, and Flash were there. We told them to get a ride and meet us on Hemlock and Sutter. We got there first and waited for our guys; they had walked, and it took them about forty minutes.

There were thirteen of us. We were charged a dollar each to get into the party, but that was OK with us. We were told that the money was going to be used to bail out the brother of the lady who owned the house; this kind of stuff was done all the time. When we got down to the basement of the house, the party was on. It was packed with guys and some very good-looking ladies; it looked like it was going to be a positive experience. A slow song was playing, "In the Still of the Night" by the Five Satins. I loved that song, so I walked right up to this cute girl and asked her if she would like to dance. At the same moment, a guy walked up to us with two drinks in his hands. He looked at me and said, "Can I help you, man?" The way he said it, I knew then that this wasn't going to be good, but if that was his lady, I had to respect him. I kindly excused myself, got myself a soda, and stood in the corner waiting for the sign, which I knew had to come before the night was over.

The beers were twenty-five cents a can. An hour hadn't gone by yet, and Sandy had already had six or seven beers. I saw Sandy walk up to the owner's husband at the door and say something to him. Much later, Sandy told us that he had said to the guy, "I don't see you charging anyone else to get in. Why were we the only guys that had to pay?" The guy had said, "These people are from the neighborhood, so they don't have to pay."

The basement had a small kitchen, a sofa, a TV, end tables, lamps, a china cabinet, and a few folding chairs on a light vinyl tile floor. Sandy was pissed and said to the guy at the door, "Me and my boys want our money back!" At the same time, Sonny walked up to us and said, "Everybody is talking about New Lots!" We were on one side of the room and everyone else was on the opposite side, close to the entrance. I saw that we were getting dirty looks, especially from the guy whose girlfriend I had asked to dance; he just kept staring at me. Hi Ho came up with a plan.

Hi Ho was nineteen years old, maybe one hundred and sixty five pounds, and was a nice Jewish boy from the Boulevard Projects who had more balls than common sense; at that time, I think we all did. One night, a few of our friends got fucked up at a nightclub in Flatbush. Hi Ho organized all the white gangs in East New York to meet at the club, and before the night was over, the bouncers were laid all over the parking lot with a few of their gang members, and the place was wrecked and closed down. I would rather have one Hi Ho battling by my side than five of any bullshit, loudmouthed wise guys; they needed numbers to stick. One of the New Lots Boys' biggest advantages over larger numbers in battle was that we never broke ranks. We were brothers; if you did break rank and ran and you came back to New Lots, you would be creeped out, which was the silent treatment, or you would have to take a smack, and you couldn't ever hang with our crew again.

Hi Ho said, "Just point at the first person to say something to us and start to laugh, and if anyone has the balls to come up to us, knock him out." It sounded like a plan. Big Davy, Sonny, Hi Ho, and Steve were sitting on the sofa, and the rest of us where standing around. It didn't take long before the guy who owned the house said, "If any of these punks from New Lots gives you a hard time, call me." So we all pointed to him and started laughing. The guy walked over and made a remark to Big Davy. Hi Ho jumped up and punched the guy in the face. Next thing we knew, Hi Ho was rolling on the ground with the owner of the house, the girls were screaming, and glass was breaking. I grabbed the guy who Hi Ho was fighting with and slammed him into the wall. My friends were now wrecking the place. Joey Jet had picked up the TV and thrown it into the cabinet; it sounded like a bomb went off! There were now quite a few people lying on the floor. Those guys didn't want any part of us! The owner of the house was yelling, "Get my baseball bat! I'm going to kill that curly-headed motherfucker!" He was pointing to Hi Ho. No one wanted to come near us! Hi Ho told the guy, "If your wife comes down here with a baseball bat, I'm going to stick it up your ass." The dude who had been giving me the dirty looks all night was gone. That was the first round.

Then came the second round, outside. None of them wanted to continue fighting, but the owner of the house had kicked them all out by then, so they had to come out and fight. We were now out in the street. Another guy whom Hi Ho had been fighting with wanted to fight him again, so Hi Ho started to take off his jacket when all of a sudden the guy went down. Hi Ho looked at this dude going down and said, "The guy went down and I didn't even have to hit him! Who's bad?" All our guys started laughing. Little did he know that when he was just about to hit that dude, Foxy had come up from behind and cracked him over the head with a beer can.

Now more guys were coming. This was their neighborhood, and they were coming from all over. There was a whole crew of new guys, running up and pulling up in cars. There were about thirty of them in the street, all looking at us. One guy in the front was staring at us like he was a real bad ass. Hi Ho walked up to him and said, "Do you have something to say?" The guy blew smoke into Hi Ho's face. Hi Ho punched him in his face, and we all ran into the street. It was on!

We were knocking guys out, and more cars were pulling up; their fathers, brothers, and uncles were coming. Guys were fighting with garbage cans, car antennas, beer cans, bats, and pipes. Joey Jet and Flash were fighting with this one big guy. Jet and Flash at that time weighed about one hundred and thirty pounds each. They were about five feet six or five feet seven, and they were not letting up on this guy. They were typical New Lots Boys, all heart, and that was one more dude off my ass. Hi Ho jumped on the guy Jet and

Flash were fighting when another dude cracked Hi Ho in the head with a stickball bat. Hi Ho turned and grabbed the bat. The dude bit Hi Ho on the hand. Hi Ho was pissed and tried to get the bat away from the guy, and then Sonny grabbed the guy, threw him down, and kicked him a couple of times in the head.

The fighting stopped for a minute. Those guys were in the middle of the street, and we were on the sidewalk, close to the house. By this time, their whole neighborhood was there. A big black Cadillac pulled up to the curb. Hi Ho walked up to the car, and as the back door was opening, he held the door open and said, "Good evening, Sir." A wise guy got out, looked at us, and said, "Get these punks from New Lots out of our fucking neighborhood now!" I had already knocked out three or four guys, and my adrenalin was at its peak; that night, my game was on. I jumped over the back door of the car and right handed that piece of shit. He fell back into the car, and the car took off. Those guys were part of the Vario family. They ran that part of East New York. Meanwhile, Sonny was in the street, and some guy had caught him in the back of the head with a beer can. Sonny was born a New Lots Boy. He was about my height and weight and naturally strong, and he was one bad ass dude who no one fucked with. The dude who hit him had made a big mistake. I just saw him go flying by, and it was on again.

Sandy had gotten hit in the head, and he was covered with blood. I was still banging away, so were Big Davy, Foxy, and all of our guys. I dropped Steve by mistake! When he went down, Sandy ran over and started banging on him. All we heard was "Hold it, hold it. It's me, Steve!" I was like "Oh shit! Sorry!" and I moved on. There were guys lying all over the street, girls were screaming, and people started yelling "The cops are coming!" Everyone ran! We ran south on Crescent Street to Blake Avenue and through the Cypress Hills Projects. When we got to the other side of the projects, we had slowed down and begun to walk when one guy who had been running with us said, "We really kicked the shit out of those guys from New Lots, huh?" We all turned and looked at this moron. We didn't have the heart to fuck him up. It seemed like we all said at the same time "Get the fuck out of here you fucking idiot!" He took off like a bullet, back through the Cypress Hills Projects, where the bros probably ate him.

Hi Ho took Sandy to the hospital where he got a few stitches in his head. Then they went back to the corner. It was about 2:00 a.m., and most of us guys had to go home. There were a few guys on the corner that weren't at the fight. Sandy was pissed off and wanted to go back again. Hi Ho, Sonny, Sandy, Ronnie, Joe M, Frenchie, Anthony L, and Richie S, all wanted to go back to Hemlock and Sutter and kick ass. I went home to lick the wounds I didn't have. It may sound strange, but when I got in to those big wars, I didn't mind catching a few; the times I did, I slept like a baby. I found out the next day that some of the guys did go back in two cars. To their surprise, there were fifteen Hemlock and Sutter dudes just hanging out. Our guys jumped out of the cars with bats and car antennas and just fucked up as many dudes as they could catch. Those dudes didn't know what hit them. When it was over, our guys went back to the Triangle.

That was a Friday night. The following Monday, Sonny's father came to the corner and asked us if we had had a fight Friday night down by Hemlock and Sutter. We said, "Ya, we did. Why?" Sonny's father worked in Manhattan on a construction crew, and guys were talking on the job about the fight, saying that the New Lots Boys had fucked up a lot of people, including a couple of wise guys. Sonny's father said, "Listen! If you fuck with these wise guys, they will shoot you!" So we went back a few times more. We didn't get shot, and the Hemlock and Sutter dudes took the beatings along with the wise guys. Those dudes were afraid to come out of their houses.

A few weeks later, a guy named John N, who Hi Ho knew from Cleveland and Fulton Street, called Hi Ho and said, "Hi Ho, you're from New Lots, do you think you can do me a favor and talk to your friends? My cousin is from Hemlock and Sutter, and he's afraid to walk out of his house." Hi Ho said, "OK, I'll see what I can do." A few days later, Hi Ho called the guy back and told him "Everything is going to be OK." The guy told Hi Ho that his cousin wanted to meet him, so Hi Ho went to their neighborhood to meet the guy's cousin. He thought the guy's cousin would be a little guy because he had been afraid to come out of his house. When he got there, he saw that the dude was over six feet tall and over two hundred pounds. There were three of them there, Patsy R, John Carneglia, whose father was also a wise guy, and the cousin of the guy who Hi Ho knew. They asked Hi Ho if they could go to New Lots Avenue and if it would be safe for them. Hi Ho said, "Ya, definitely! If my people say it's cool, you can take them at their word."

It was a weeknight when they got to New Lots. Most of the older guys were hanging on the corner. They parked their cars and they asked Hi Ho "Where are your friends?" He said, "Probably in the Boy's Club." The East New York Boy's Club was on Ashford Street, a few feet off New Lots Avenue. So they walked into the Boy's Club, and all they saw were guys boxing, lifting weights, and wrestling on the mats. John Carneglia looked at Hi Ho and said, "You guys are like fucking gladiators!" After that, we became good friends and found out that most of them were really nice guys.

That side of East New York inspired the book by Nicholas Pileggi called *Wiseguy* and the movie *Goodfellas*. Hollywood portrays those people as stand-up guys, which was the farthest thing from the truth. Most of the top guys thought that they were bigger than life and were self-promoting and caught up in the media hype; it always ended in their demise. Take Henry Hill, this is what I can tell you about that piece of shit, he started out as a gofer for the Varios and ended up as a rat and a Hollywood opportunist.

New Lots Boys versus the Monster Bro

It was the fall of 1961. I had just left some of the guys on New Lots Avenue. It wasn't late, but I was tired and had to go to work early the next day. I was walking south on Elton Street on my way home. I was just about to cross Hegeman Avenue, on the northwest corner next to Minnie's Bar, when I heard the New Lots warning whistle. I knew that meant someone from New Lots was in trouble.

I turned without seeing anyone and began running back to New Lots Avenue. Yes, we had a New Lots whistle. We got it from Johnny Reb and his rebels. When I got to the corner of Elton Street and New Lots Avenue, the first guy I saw was Bruno. He was chasing this huge black dude that he just caught up to. The bro had a long pipe in his hand.

I didn't know it at that time, but there were four bros trying to rob Schneider's Jewish Deli. Sonny and a few of the guys caught the other three bros on Cleveland Street and New Lots Avenue. I came at the guy Bruno had caught up to. This guy was a monster; he was swinging the pipe, and we couldn't get at him. He kept swinging, and we kept backing off. He was taking these big long swings. I had to get to this piece of shit, so I timed his swings and ran in. I climbed straight up that mountain. I had him now, I thought for just a second. He had the pipe in his right hand and me like a rag doll in the other. This was one big fucking dude, I mean, Mr. Dude! I was holding him as close to me as I could, holding him with my left hand and banging him with my right hand. I had my legs around the top part of his legs. Bruno was trying to rip the pipe out of his hand, but this fucking guy wasn't budging; as long as he held on to that pipe, our asses were in jeopardy. This was one dangerous man, even without the pipe. My mind was racing! We were in front of two billboards that were in a small empty lot. There was nothing to pick up and use as a weapon. Across the street was a butcher shop, the Modern Meat Market. To the right, there was a small A&P grocery store, and to the right of that was Benny's Luncheonette.

Now Bruno was one of the toughest guys I knew, and I could also bang with both hands, fast and strong. In those days, Bruno, Jerry, another real tough guy, and I would go down to Jerry's basement, lift weights, hit the heavy bag, then spar in a nasty street-fighting style. In other words, we would just kick the shit out of one another, in an anything-goes style. The only difference between us was Jerry was fast and strong, a little lighter in weight and shorter than Bruno or me. Now Bruno and I were just about the same size and were just about even in our skills; the only advantage I had was that he was a really nice guy. Not that I wasn't when I was off the court, but when I was on the court (street), I wanted to hurt you, and my biggest advantage was I wasn't afraid to die trying.

I tripped the monster up, and he went down. He tried to get up again and again while we were still throwing punches. This wasn't working. He wouldn't stay down! He took a big deep breath and stood straight up. Bruno tripped him again, and he fell forward. We just couldn't keep him down. I ran across the street to Benny's Luncheonette. There were always milk crates outside; they were made of hard wood and metal. I grabbed one and ran back across the street to where Bruno was still at it. The monster was just about up again. I ran up to this monster and cracked him in the head at least four or five times. That was when he loosened up on the pipe just enough so that I could grab it. I took a hold of the pipe and cracked him in the head a few more times with it. Believe it or not, this fucking terror got to his feet and ran. Blood was all over the place. I looked at Bruno and said, "What the fuck was that?" He was gone, and I was glad. Sonny and the other guys had two of the bros spread out facedown in the middle of New Lots Avenue. After it was all over, Mr. Schneider came running out, shaking and yelling at us. At first I couldn't understand what he was saying, and I was thinking, "He should be thanking us" What I was hearing I couldn't believe. Here he was yelling at us and telling us to mind our own business. He kept saying over and over again, "Now they're going to come back, and what am I going to do?" I couldn't understand, and I still don't. We must treat one another with justice and have moral courage. More important than losing my life is to lose my spirit. (If you kill me in battle, that would be my true reward.)

New Lots Boys versus Big Gene and Charlie

At fourteen, I started to hang out with the New Lots Boys at Elton Street Park, at the Triangle, sometimes at the PS 202 school yard, and on some nights across the street from the school, at Izzy's candy store on the corner of Atkins and Hegeman Avenues. There I met another Italian East New York beauty named Diane, with dark shiny brown hair, big dark brown eyes, a dark olive complexion, and a kick ass body; this was one beautiful young lady. Our relationship didn't last long because she was a flirt and a big pain in the ass, and I was still on my journey.

It was 1961, I'm sixteen. It was a cold dark December night. Izzy called me and a couple of the guys over to ask if we were looking for work. There was me, the Mick, George Two Way, and Raoul. He told us that there was a company next door called Consumer Carpets, and the owner, Harry Scullnick, had asked him if he knew any kids in the neighborhood who wanted to work. I was looking for a change from my Uncle Frank's butcher shop. We all said yes. The only stipulation was that we each had to buy Izzy a pint of whiskey, and he then made the introductions. We met Harry the next day. He looked at all of us and told us we were too skinny and that we should understand that it was only for a few months; he needed us just for the season from September till the end of December. He said he would pay $60 for a five-day work week for us to be helpers to his carpet mechanics. At that time, I was making $40 for six days working with my uncle, so this sounded really good to me. He explained what he needed us to do. I asked, "When can we start?" It was a Friday afternoon, so he said that the week was over and to come in on Monday morning. Harry had two large accounts for carpet installations: Macy's and Gimbal's department stores in Manhattan. Everything sounded great to me. My uncle didn't need me because his business was very slow, and he had another friend of mine, Richie, who worked there. So on Monday morning, I went to work. It was a great day. I worked with Tipper and Louie in an apartment in Kew Gardens, Queens, New York. They were two great guys to work with, and they were only about twenty-two or twenty-three years old, just starting to go out on their own. This was for me. After a few months, the season was over, but Harry kept us on. I was paired up with the only black guy in the shop, Bonnie. He was from British Honduras, like I knew were British Honduras was. He was a soft-spoken young man in his midtwenties. He was the carpet installer, and I was his helper. We went to work every day, and not having much in common, we hardly would say a word to each other. I learned his every move, and we became the power crew. Then one morning, I went to meet Bonnie at the shop. While I was waiting for Bonnie to pick up the work for the day, I sat in the entrance with the other helpers while the installers picked up their work. There were about forty guys in the building. There were about six of us helpers from New Lots, and the shop was in the New Lots section of Brooklyn. My friend, the Mick, walked in and told us he had a problem with Charlie and Gene on the job yesterday. Charlie was in his midtwenties, about my size, and Gene was about eighteen and a pretty big guy. I had just turned sixteen and still trained hard every night. The Mick was a little guy, about five feet six, kind of light in the ass, but it didn't stop him. He told us that Gene broke his balls all day the day before and blamed the Mick for stealing his sharpening stone, and he would call the Mick "sunshine" just to break his balls. Charlie and Gene weren't in the shop yet, so I told the Mick, "When they get here, if Gene calls you 'sunshine' again, just call him a fat fuck." A few minutes went by and then Charlie and Gene came in, walking through us and laughing like we were pieces of shit. As soon as Gene got up to where the Mick was standing, he looked down at the Mick and said, "Hey, sunshine, where the fuck is my stone?" The Mick said, "I don't have your stone, you fat motherfucker!" Gene grabbed the Mick and threw him on the floor, but before he got one shot off, I was on him, banging him with lefts and rights, punching him till he hit the ground. Charlie had jumped on my back. I pulled him off me like he was a paper doll, right handed him, and he went right to sleep. Gene was staring up at me. I could see in his eyes he was done. Harry ran over to us, grabbed me, and said, "Richie, you just knocked out two of my installers. I need them." I told Harry in the heat of the moment "This is New Lots, motherfucker, and if you want to stay in business, you better talk to these scumbags!" Harry said, "I will. Just take it easy and go with Bonnie to work." I turned and looked at Charlie and Gene; they were still on the floor. I told them that if they ever thought of fucking with any of us again, we would go to their fucking houses and whip their asses again. They never said a word. I got in the car with Bonnie. Bonnie was in shock, but I could see that he was proud. He said, "I thought you were so quiet!" I said, "I am," and we broke out laughing. I never knew what he thought about me, the only white kid willing to work with him, and I never complained, and why would I? He taught me how to install carpet the right way; that was my future, thanks to Bonnie. A few weeks later, I went to see my friend Ira. He had a carpet store on Liberty Avenue. He had gone to Franklin K Lane High school. I told him about the fight I had at Consumer Carpets with those two guys, Charlie and Gene. When I mentioned Gene's last name, he looked surprised and told me that Gene and his brother were two bad ass dudes in high school.

Again, I worked at fighting. I decided what was in my best interest then acted upon it. Those were the days when one's family, friends, and neighborhood meant something to you, and you could be proud of them and loyal. It built your character and style and the way you carried yourself. Your dress code showed you and told people that you had pride in yourself. Your causal style would be cotton chino pants with that small short buckle belt in the back and an iron crease in the front or a neat pair of blue jeans with no holes. Your mother would press freshly cleaned cotton shirts or a cool Italian knit shirt. Add buck skin shoes or Converse, Keds, or PF Flyers sneakers. On Friday and Saturday nights, you dressed in an Italian knit sweater, mohair or sharkskin suit, French toe, or featherweight shoes with a high spit shine. I shopped for dress clothes at Buddy Lee in downtown Brooklyn; at Royal Fashion, on East Nineteenth Street in Manhattan; or at Kings Highway in Brooklyn. Likely, your dad had a Ford or a Chevy car. You would listen to Murray the K or Night Train on the radio. When I transferred from East New York Vocational High School, where you had to dress in slacks, shirt, and tie, to the more social and liberal Thomas Jefferson High School, where you were allowed to dress down, with old faded ripped jeans and a T-shirt, I knew I didn't want to be there. I invented the lie to myself that life and times were great, and for me it really seemed to be, but the real world started to take effect all around me. I kept up with my passion, training hard for my next contest, not ignoring what was coming; but as a child of the fifties, I had no knowledge of the human jungle and the social alien invasion creeping into East New York.

New Lots Boys versus Puerto Rican Turf: Round 2

It was the summer of 1962. Foxy had called me on a Saturday night and asked, "Q, do you want to go to the feast tonight?" I said, "Where are you?" He told me he was calling from the Triangle. I said I'd be there in a half an hour. It was a nice night, and I was in the mood for a sausage and pepper hero. Walking from the Triangle to St. Rita's feast was pretty much against the laws of nature for young white boys, but we walked north, up Essex Street. I'm not going to lie to you; I had a tension inside me. The good thing was that it kept me alert and sharp. We got to the feast without incident.

As soon as we walked into the feast, we could smell the sausages and peppers. So the first stand Foxy and I went to was for our sausage and pepper sandwich. None of our guys were there, so we hung out with a few of the guys from Highland Park, Bobby Bear and his crew. Bobby Bear was out of his mind. He was a bad dude with a set of balls to match, a real East New York character. Most of the so-called tough guys from East New York would just pay lip service, but not Bobby Bear. He was a warrior, a crazy fuck. I liked his character. We hung out for a while. Not much was happening. We met up with a few of the guys from Liberty Park. They told me and Foxy that they had had trouble the night before on Sutter Avenue and Elton Street and that the PRs were all over Sutter Avenue fucking with every white dude that tried to cross the street. The guys from Liberty Park said that they might go back that night. Foxy and I said, "Let us know." We stayed about an hour longer, played a couple of games, and decided to go back to New Lots.

We headed south, down Linwood Street. When we got to Sutter Avenue, as we were crossing the street, we heard yelling from one block west of where we were. We were on Linwood Street in the middle of Sutter Avenue. There was a fight going on the north side of Elton Street and Sutter Avenue. The guys from Liberty Park were fighting with the PRs again. Foxy said, "Let's go help the guys from Liberty Park." We got halfway up Sutter Avenue when the Liberty Park guys split; I guess the PRs were prepared and the Liberty Park guys were way outnumbered. Foxy still wanted to go. I grabbed his arm and told him to stop, which he did. Next thing we knew, the PRs turned and were coming at us. Foxy was still ready to get down. One of us had to get this right, and I knew that if we stayed there one more minute, it wasn't going to work out good for us. I told Foxy to follow me. We turned and ran east on Sutter Avenue, then south on Linwood Street. As soon as we turned the corner, I grabbed Foxy and told him to pick up a metal garbage can. I grabbed a two-by-four that was lying there. We were on the southwest corner of Linwood Street and Sutter Avenue. There was a brick apartment building on the corner. I told Foxy to get against the wall and so did I. When the PRs came around the corner, thinking we were still running, the first three or four that turned the corner ran right into Foxy's metal garbage can and my two by four. They were down! The rest of them stopped dead in their tracks. We backed off and threw down our weapons. At the same time, we both said, "New Lots, motherfuckers." We turned and jogged back to New Lots, laughing our asses off. A couple of nights later, Foxy was coming home from the feast when he got jumped and hit in the forehead with a pipe. When he got to the Triangle, he had this huge bump on his head. I had never seen a bump that big; it looked freaky. There were a few of us on the corner. We were pissed, and we were going to go back to Sutter Avenue. Foxy said he wanted to go. I said, "What the fuck is wrong with you? You can't go! Go look in the fucking mirror." I took him into the Triangle restroom. He took one look at his forehead, and I thought he was going to pass out. I said, "We can go to the hospital, or you can go home." He said, "Ya, that sounds like a good idea. I've got a bad headache. I'm going home." I said, "We won't go back tonight without you. Let's give you a couple of days to heal. They're not going anywhere." By this time, my attitude was making a difference in my life, and it was making an impact on the people around me. That's when I decided to walk anywhere I wanted, even in the areas I shouldn't. The next night, Flash's girlfriend, Gertrud, asked me to walk her home. She lived on Essex Street, between Sutter and Belmont Avenues, not a good area to show my face. Kraute, this German guy, and Richie S said, "Is it OK if we go with you? We were going to go to the feast anyway." Little did they know that I wasn't the guy you wanted to walk through this neighborhood with. I said "OK, but I want to tell you guys to follow me and do whatever I do." We were walking from New Lots Avenue going north, up Essex Street. As we got closer to Sutter Avenue, PRs were coming out of their houses and off their stoops, gathering in the street behind us. We kept walking across Sutter

Avenue. When we got across the street, I told Gertrud to run home. I told Richie and Kraute to follow me. I turned around. There were about thirty PRs in the middle of Sutter Avenue. I said, "That's right, motherfuckers, New Lots!" I could tell that they were ready to make their move when this black minister came out from of a storefront church on the corner. He stood in between us and said, "Let's not fight, boys." There was another girl I knew, Nina, and she was sitting on her stoop right in front of us. She yelled, "Q, you better run! There are more guys coming!" I said, "Watch me, girl!" As one PR pushed the minister out of the way, I cracked him with a straight right hand, knocking him into the minister. I told Richie and Kraute again to follow me, and I turned and ran. I turned to look back; Kraute never ran, he froze. I grabbed a metal garbage can and ran back, swinging the garbage can. I yelled to Kraute to get the fuck out of there. We turned and ran. The PRs were in hot pursuit.

On Essex Street from Sutter to Belmont Avenue, there were two-story row houses with small front yards, on both sides of the street, and every yard had at least two or three metal garbage cans. Halfway up the block, I grabbed a garbage can and ran back south on Essex Street, swinging the garbage can. The PRs backed off! At that, I threw the can at them and continued to do it again and again until I had every garbage can on both sides of the street in the middle of the street. That was when I turned and split. We went to the feast. Richie said, "What the fuck was that?" With an expressionless face, I said, "That there gave me an immediate intoxicating effect, and I love it." He just shook his head. We walked through the feast then went home without incident. The next night, I went to the Triangle. The night was nice. There were about fifty guys hanging out on the corner, the older guys and the younger guys. One of the older guys, Nicky, my friend Louie's cousin, asked if any of us guys had a fight on Essex Street last night. I said, "Ya, I did!" He laughed and said that every garbage can was in the middle of the street. I said, "I left a few PRs lying there too." Nicky lived on that block and worked for the sanitation department. I said, "Nicky, when I'm eighteen, would this qualify me for a job with the sanitation department?" He said, "I don't think so," and we had a good laugh. (By now, I knew that my house was on fire. I never thought for a second I could extinguish it. Looking back to my inner feelings, I never felt hate. I understood the moment, but I didn't yet understand the times.)

Diane & Jr.

Dutch Reform Church and Graveyard

St. Gabrielle Church

Left: Richie Q—Right: Hi Ho

Charlie Tarzan

Foxy—aka Lord Fox—Vietnam

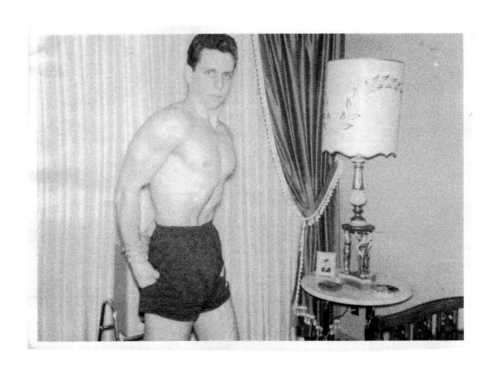

Hi Ho

Hi Ho

Bobby Bear

REGINALD A. NERO

Left Photo—Mr. Nero & Richie Q.

New Lots Boys—Coney Island—
Top Back Row Starting from Left: Sal—Walter—Foxy—Big Davey—Tony—Jerry
Center Row Starting from Left: Richie Q—Lee—Bruno—Georgie—Charlie Tarzan
Bottom Row—Louie

New Lots Boys—Coney Island

New Lots Boys

New Lots Boys

You can go out and stomp for joy
But no one stomps on a
New Lots Boy

Calling Card

New Lots Boys

New Lots Boys

New Lots Boys Arsonal

Richie Q—Fort Dix

Fort Dix
Left: Walter—Right: Richie Q

Starting Left Top: Lil Joe—Center Top: Patsy P—
Right Top: Georgie—Center Front: The Mick

Envelope from Foxy—Vietnam

Dear Mrs. Quarentallio,   1/13/67

I haven't heard from Richie since th[...] him.
I am still aw[...] a reply [...] my last letter. Try not to worry to m[...] because he doesn't write.

When they're in the [...] they don't get too much time for things [...]. I don't even write home that much. In fact, today's l[...] to my mother is the first in about 1½ weeks.

I don't know, we don't mean not to write. But we just don't know what to write about.

Richie is looking terrific. He wears a black beret, cause he is a Recon Commando. Believe me you have a lot to be proud of, about Richie. He's one in a million.

The scars that he had from the wounds are mine. He has one on his leg, that is 4" long.

Page 1 Ltr Foxy—Vietnam

II

Then he has one on his behind
& leg, that are very small + no one
will be able to see, because his shorts
cover them.

Seeing Richie over here is the
best thing that I could have asked for.
We spent about 2½ days together.

In some ways it was just
like old times, cause I was broke +
your kind hearted son Richie was
treating me again.

We went down to Saigon,
+ we had a little fun. Don't worry I
made sure he didn't get in any trouble.
But mostly we talked about old times +
what we thought the future foretold
for us.

He's the same old Richie,
looking as good as ever + conceited as
ever. I hate to go out with him cause
I don't have a chance with him around.
He must be doing something right.

Page 2 Ltr from Foxy—Vietnam

III

Well try & not worry, cause he'll be home at the end of april. Which is now 3 months away.

I can't explain how I felt when we had to part each other. With Richie going back + me staying here. I would now & then give anything to be right by his side. I only wish that we would of, gone through this together.

Few parents are as fortunate as you + your husband to have such a son. There is only one Richie Q, + there will always only be one.

Well that's about it. Don't worry he'll be back before you know it. Say hello to your husband + Day-Day + Frank -+ marie + espicially little Frankie.

Until I'm back in your house convincing Richie to be a bad boy.

Love Ya's always

Lonnie
(Fox)

Page 3 Ltr from Foxy—Vietnam

Richie Q

Rockaways Playland

Richie Q forth from Left Top—New Lots Boys and Girls

Richie Q Butcher Bike

Young New Lots Boys—Richie Q basement

Young New Lots Girls

My Mom (Josie), Dad (Domonic), Brother and Richie Q as a baby

Elton Street Park

Jojo

New Lots Boys versus the Saints

It was the summer of 1962. The Saints, like the Chaplains, the largest black street gang in Brooklyn, New York, were the largest street gang in Queens, New York. Their members consisted of black, white, and Puerto Ricans. I was seventeen and pretty much established in my natural ability. It was a beautiful, summer Sunday morning. I had a good work week, and I had money in my pocket. I had gotten up early. I could smell my mother cooking bacon and eggs. She said, "Come on, get up! The coffee is made." I had gotten up early every morning since age eleven. I've always been a morning person. I had my breakfast, took a shower, and got dressed in a pair of jeans, a new white T-shirt, and a pair of tan buck skin shoes.

If I wasn't working or working out, I would start my day or night with my friends on New Lots Avenue. At that age, we had already merged with the older guys. Our crew was the toughest crew New Lots ever had; we'd been through dozens of wars. When I got to New Lots Avenue, Hi Ho, Arnie, Foxy, Schmitty and his Schmidt mobile, an old blue station wagon, and a few more of our guys were hanging out, all looking for something to do. I for one couldn't let this day go to waste. Hi Ho said, "I bet you half of East New York is at the beach."

There were two beaches; the first was on Ninety-Eight Street, the Rockaway Beach, where almost everyone from East New York would go, from the older guys and girls to the younger boys and girls; and the second was on Thirty-Fifth Street, the Far Rockaway Beach, a new beach where a lot of the younger guys and girls, mostly in their mid-teens, would go. We decided to go to Thirty-Fifth Street. Everyone agreed, so we jumped in the Schmidt mobile and headed to Far Rockaway. Thirty-Fifth Street was about forty-five minutes from New Lots Avenue, south on Cross Bay Boulevard, across the first bridge, ten minutes to the second bridge, a left turn when you got over the second bridge, and another ten minutes to Thirty-Fifth Street.

We pulled into the parking lot across the street from the boardwalk. I felt great. I knew there would be some of the prettiest girls from Brooklyn and Queens, and I was sure all eight of us were thinking the same thing. We couldn't get out of the Schmidt mobile fast enough. We ran across the street and up a ramp onto the boardwalk. Walking down the ramp were two beautiful young ladies. I knew this was going to be a good day. We had just about stepped on to the boardwalk when we heard cheering and yelling, "New Lots is here!" About twenty guys from East New York were on the boardwalk. Bobby Bear, the leader of Highland Park and one of the baddest guys in East New York; Babe Costanza, another bad ass guy from Liberty Park; Paulie C from Fountain and Pitkin; guys from Hemlock and Sutter; and the Crescent Street guys were all there. Together it looked like there were a hundred guys from East New York. I was seventeen years old at that time. We had been fighting against one another since I was fourteen. I got to know mostly all of these guys by then. I knew the guys who would stand up and the guys that were all talk. This is how I felt—we could fuck with one another, but if someone outside East New York fucked with any one from East New York, we stood together. Pauli C ran up to us. There was a break in his voice when he said, "The Saints were just here and we had it out, and they said they will be coming back! Half of them went for reinforcements, and the other half are in that bar."

On the boardwalk, about a hundred feet from where we were standing, there was a small bar and a few game stores. I personally had never had a run in with the Saints. I only heard about the Saints once before. One of the guys from Fountain and Pitkin, Eddie M, had gotten jumped and stabbed and lost a lung. So I knew this wasn't going to be a walk in the park. There were nearly a hundred guys from East New York, and some of them were toughest guys I knew. I could feel the physical intenseness in these guys. So what do I do? Without a word, I walked right to the bar. Arnie was on my left side, and I knew that Hi Ho and the rest of the guys were right behind me. There were two dudes standing outside the bar. As I walked up, they looked at one another like to say "no big deal." One of the guys was about my size with a placid indifference on his face. I knew why he felt that way; the dude standing next to him was huge, and you could see he was in good shape. His face was cold, with prominent cheekbones and intense eyes. He had a red bandana on his head, and he was covered with jailhouse tattoos. He definitely had the formula to be one bad guy! He kind of reminded me of the Rogue, Robbie the Rogue, just about the baddest guy in East New York, or all of Brooklyn at that time.

Robbie was about six years older than I was and originally from Crescent Street. He began hanging out at the Triangle in 1961. He was about six feet four and spent most of his life in jail for petty theft and drugs. Quite a number of my friends were in jail with him at one time or another and told stories of Robbie being the baddest dude, black or white. No one fucked with him, inside and outside the ring, whether in jail or on the street. He was the heavyweight champ. I could picture him standing on the corner in the summer with a bandana on his head, wearing shorts, and his bull dog Jake by his side. He was the first guy I ever heard of that did heroin. I liked the guy. He had the most corrupt mind and a quiet fury, an out of place character without any social values. The Rogue was a nice guy to talk to. He was knowledgeable. I once asked him why, and he said in his absolute opinion, even if you are the most evil of sinners, in the end, we all cross over.

When I was nineteen years old and he knew at that time I was going to Vietnam, he was the first person to thank me for my service. I measured myself and harbored doubt about a war with Robbie; again, I worked every day at those possibilities. If I was unsure of success in my street war, I knew that even if I fought to my death, that person would be damaged for life, body and mind. Was this dude my Robbie the Rogue?

As he looked down at me with those eyes, I knew one thing; if I get off first, I'm going to hurt this guy. As I walked up to these two, without a word, I hit the big dude with a vicious right hand. As he went back staggering into the bar, I followed up with two more quick right hands before he hit the ground. The big dude was done, and I never found out if he was a bad ass.

By this time in my life, I found a lot of big guys that looked bad and tough hardly ever got into street wars and never had the beneficial achievement or the struggle. Now I was in the bar. I looked up, and every guy in the bar was on me. I backed out, throwing lefts and rights. Arnie stood toe to toe with me, banging everyone that exited the bar. When I heard Hi Ho yell "Q!" I turned to look. East on the boardwalk, as far as I could see, there were guys running at us with bats, pipes, and chains. We backed off then stood and held our ground. All the guys from East New York came up onto the boardwalk. I said, "Fuck it!" and ran right into this maze of horrific chaos, banging as I moved forward, knowing in this heat that I had the wisdom, knowledge, and discipline from mistakes I had made in the past to keep my reserve by banging with lefts and right, keeping these dogs off balance. There were so many Saints, and more and more were coming. They were backing us up now. We backed up to Thirty-Sixth Street and held our ground. I remember fighting with two guys against the rail on the beach side of the boardwalk, and Pauli was fighting with a guy next to me. The guy he was fighting picked him up and threw him over the metal railing on to the beach.

I had one guy in front of me and the other on my back. I threw the guy on my back over the railing; the other guy was the smaller of the two guys that were outside the bar, so I would guess at that point he knew I was the guy that knocked out his creature. He turned and jumped over the rail onto the beach. I went right after him. He hit the sand, jumped up, and ran down the beach. I hit the sand, and there was Pauli with five or six girls yelling "Pauli, are you OK?" I said, "He's OK. Come on, let's go." We both ran up the steps, back on to the boardwalk, and into the battle, the fire. I had never seen so many guys at war, and if I didn't recognize you, I was banging. After a while, I found myself fading from the heat and burning sun.

They had superior manpower and weapons. I hated to admit it, but I don't think we could have lasted much longer. Next thing I heard were the faint sound of sirens in the distance. They were getting closer and louder, and I knew it would be over soon. For some reason, I got a second wind. All I remember is having the desire, the passion, and the actual pleasure. I knew how to do this, and I liked doing it. The first cop to hit the boardwalk was this short, stocky dude with a homely face and a beet-red complexion. He was running right for me. I was still banging, and he was about three feet from me. I just dropped the guy I was fighting and looked up, and there he was in my face, just as one of the Saints was running past me. I stepped to the left and left hooked the Saint. He fell to my right, and officer homely and this dude were down. I split and jumped over the rail and into the parking lot. The Schmidt mobile was already moving. I jumped in and we were off. All our guys were OK. We headed back to New Lots, hurrying past cop car after cop car. By the time we got to Cross Bay Boulevard, we knew the law was behind us, and we were filled with exhilarating pleasure.

That night, Hi Ho had told me that he went up to Highland Park looking for Bobby Bear. When he got to Atlantic Avenue, between Elton and Linwood Streets, he met up with two brothers that were at the fight. They were hanging on their stoop with friends and family. Their mother thanked Hi Ho for saving her sons. Hi Ho had told me that this guy with a heavy belt buckle had cracked one brother then the other. Hi Ho had jumped on the guy, throwing him down and banging his head on the boardwalk. They told Hi Ho that a lot of guys from East New York got banged up pretty badly; a few guys got stabbed and sliced, but our guys were pretty lucky. I measure myself by the man I am and who I have become. You have to have the courage to work through your fears. I am still bent on serving the folly, my battle of life.

Two weeks after that war, we went back to Thirty-Fifth Street, Hi Ho, Charlie Tarzan, Foxy, me, and a few of the guys from Fountain and Pitkin. We took the train, but there wasn't much happening, so we decided to walk back to the train and take it up to Ninety-Eighth Street. The train was about twenty feet above ground, with a chain link fence on two sides. You had to cross a narrow two-way street with cars parked on one side and the chain link fence on the other. We all crossed the street and walked along the fence heading for the entrance to the train when these guys in their car came driving down the street, getting so close and almost hitting Hi Ho and Foxy. Foxy yelled, "You motherfucker." The car stopped and made a U-turn, heading back at us. We were pinned against the fence with nowhere to go. There, coming in the opposite direction, was a city bus. These guys were now on the wrong side of the road. By the time they saw the bus and tried to turn out of its way, it was too late. On that narrow street, as they turned, they hit a parked car on the other side of the street and turned completely over on its roof, with gas leaking and four tires spinning up, right in the middle of the street. I ran up to where the driver was trying to crawl out. As he got halfway out, I kicked him in the face. I bent down, pulled him out, and cracked him a couple of times. He was done. The guys from Fountain and Pitkin grabbed the dude out of the backseat window, and he was done too. Foxy and Hi Ho had run to the other side of the car and laid a beating on the guy trying to crawl out the passenger side window.

As we started to run for the stairs to the train station, the people in the bus and on the sidewalk were looking at us in shock, like we were animals. We ran up the stairs. From the train platform, you could look down and see the chaos in the street and cop cars approaching. We got lucky! The moment the train pulled up, we got on and headed back to East New York, and we were eager to get there. No matter what you think (yeah, you), I found delight, joy, and contentment within myself. I found a reward in the result. By this time in my life, the New Lots Boys were allied with every white gang in East New York. The only exception were the older guys from Fulton and Rockaway; their interest were clear: crime and money. Their younger crew our age were mostly on drugs; the few that weren't were delivered by the fathers, older brothers, uncles, and cousins into that dead end world of crime. I kept growing and feeling good about myself. I was healthy and having fun. I had everything I needed plus an unselfish devotion to the New Lots Boys. All my friends seemed to have that same spirit. All my values and principles were clear, mostly emotional, and there was no faking reality.

My fire was still burning. I hung out for the rest of that day on New Lots Avenue with Hi Ho, Foxy, CharlieTarzan, and a few of our crew and some of the older guys from the corner. That night, I walked home feeling good. I walked down New Lots Avenue to Elton Street, made a right, and walked south past Elton Street Park. It was late, and the park was quiet. The night had this warm, calming effect on me; there was a full moon and a light warm breeze on my face. From Hegeman Avenue to Stanly Avenue on my left was a huge concrete wall that housed the trains. On Linden Boulevard, there was a tunnel held up by large concrete pillars. As I crossed Stanly Avenue, there was this large oak tree; its branches always seemed to be reaching for me and welcoming me safely back home. There were many nights like this one for me to think and clear my mind and experience my awareness as East New York was being dragged through the muck. I always welcome those nights.

New Lots Boys versus Fort Green Chaplains

It was a beautiful summer's night in 1962. I was seventeen years old. At this time in my life, I was pretty much at the top of my fight game and feeling pure contentment, and most of my experiences aligned with my values. I came home from work and took a shower. My mother had made a white fish fillet dinner, with mixed greens and mashed potatoes. It was a Friday night; not that we were practicing Catholics, but we still held to some Catholic traditions, like no meat on Friday. After dinner, I got dressed in a pair of black chino cotton slacks, a white guinea T-shirt, a pair of black leather gum sole shoes, and a brand-new off-white light summer jacket. I thought I would walk to New Lots and see what the guys were doing. When I got to the corner, there were only a few of the older guys hanging out. Bush and his dad were hanging out; they were great guys, and both were dressed up, looking good, and just hanging. I said, "Did you see any of my friends?" They said, "No, but some of the younger guys were going to a party on the corner of New Lots and Shepherd Avenues." I always liked the younger guys, Lil Joe, Vinnie, Carl, Papo, Tony, and Robert; they had the cutest girls. Back in those days, you had to respect the girls. I was a lot older than they were, by at least two or three years, which made a big difference. I found the party. It was in someone's cellar. I hung out for about an hour. I was about to leave when a couple of the girls asked me if I would walk them home. The girls, Connie, her sister, and their friend Cathy, were three little cuties. Connie and her sister lived on Schenck Avenue, just off New Lots, about half a mile from the corner, across the street from the Old Dutch Reform Church. It was a beautiful night for a walk.

East New York was now in a free fall, a war zone with no rules. The political system in New York wanted no part of East New York, and it was their personal dumping ground for the low to middle class and a community of mostly blue-collar working class. They dumped people from outside New York, either looking for work when East New York was pretty much depleted of jobs or people with no income or on welfare. This caused a meltdown, and they never took responsibility for the riots, muggings of seniors, rapes, stick ups, and burglaries. With no rules or consequences, most of the cops at the Seventy-Fifth Precinct were corrupt, and the ones that weren't just did their job and didn't give a shit. Not that I could blame them, but the top cops and politicians were afraid of the R word (Racism). They knew it could kill their career, so they turned a blind eye, and the cops that gave a shit had to fight their daily wars with one hand tied behind their backs.

We had just walked past the cemetery next to the Dutch Reform Church, where some of the original Dutch settlers were buried. We were just passing the Church when a few of the younger New Lots Boys came running east on New Lots Avenue from Hendrix Street. As they got closer to us, I grabbed the first guy and asked, "What's going on?" Lil Joe said, "Run, Q. We're being chased by niggers!" As they passed me, I saw about fifteen bros turn the corner at Hendrix Street and New Lots Avenue. I told the girls to run home. We were now on the corner of Schenck Avenue and New Lots. I told Lil Joe, "We're on New Lots Avenue; you don't run!" The bros caught up with us, and apparently they knew Lil Joe. The lead guy said, "Hey, Joey, you're lucky you stopped." (Lil Joe was the only one of his friends that stayed, and he could handle himself.) I said, "He's lucky, motherfucker!" and threw the lead guy a right hand. Next thing I knew, I got hit hard in my back. They had bats and pipes. I was banging with both hands. I was strong, lean, and quick; anywhere I hit you, I hurt you. I was knocking guys down and feeling no pain; I was so high on life! Again, I took a hard shot on my left side, and I thought I got hit with a bat or a pipe. I was still banging, but I knew something was wrong. I felt myself getting weak. I grabbed one of the bros, threw him up against an iron fence, and laid into him. The other bros couldn't get out of their own way fast enough trying to get a piece of me; they were in their typical feeding frenzy when they had the numbers. Now I knew something was really very wrong; I was fading fast. I ran for a metal garbage can, picked it up, and started wailing, cracking bros that were still trying to get to me. After the first two went down, the rest of them turned and ran. I had laid out more than a few bros. I was standing in the middle of New Lots Avenue, holding a metal garbage can, and a lady on the top floor of a two-story building opened her window and yelled at me, "Stop making trouble here, you!" I turned, looked up at her, and threw the garbage can at the window saying, "Kiss my fucking ass!"

Now I knew I was hurt. I just didn't know where or how badly. I was standing in the middle of the street when Connie, her sister, and Cathy ran up to me and told me that the back of my jacket was drenched with blood. Connie took me to her house. I took off my jacket and T-shirt; they were soaked with blood! Now I knew why I was getting weak. I had gotten stabbed on my left side and on my back! The cops came to Connie's house, and I was sitting on a chair when they came in with two black guys for me to identify. I didn't know for sure if they were the guys, and I didn't care. It was another street war to me, and most of the time, the cops were part of the problem, not the solution. They would make a big deal out of it by going to court four or five times. You would have to take off from work and lose money; you may even have had to hire your own lawyer, costing you more money. I didn't need these guys knowing my name or where I lived, and in New York City, they gave your information right up.

The city politicians evaded any responsibility for the miserable conditions they created. Oh ya, one big difference between the white and the black gangs of New York was that the black guys would pick out any white person in a line up, guilty or not; if he was white, that was enough.

By this time, the ambulance had shown up at the house, and it took me to Brookdale Hospital on Linden Boulevard and Rockaway Parkway. My mother and father were out for the night at the Aqueduct Racetrack.

My cousin Tony told the people at the hospital that he was my older brother because I was underage. They took me straight into emergency, without x-rays. The doctor stitched me up and sent me home. When I got home, my mom and dad and about twenty of my friends were at my house. We went next door to my uncle Frank and aunt Day Day's (her nickname) house. It was about two o'clock in the morning. My friends and I went into my aunt and uncle's house and sat in the kitchen. My friends were out for blood! I was tired and feeling like shit when my cousin Sonny came running in from outside yelling, "There are a couple of Puerto Ricans trying to rob Joey's car!" Joey lived right across the street from me. My friends ran out! Naturally, I crawled out to watch from the stoop. One guy was under the hood, probably looking to steal the battery, unaware of what was about to go down. There were two other guys standing, watching him. The two guys looked up and saw twenty angry white guys running right at them; they just turned and ran. The one poor bastard under the hood had no idea his friends had split and never saw them coming. When they got up to him and pulled him down, they saw he was just a kid, so they smacked him around a little, kicked him in the ass, and sent him on his way. I'm sure he felt lucky he didn't get a beating and that no one called the cops. I'm sure till this day they are still wondering where all those guys came from at two or three in the morning. The next day, my friends went after the bros. That night, they went and laid out more than a few bros on Warwick Street in retaliation.

I was wasted and went next door to my own house. I was now in a lot of pain. I tried to lie down on my stomach; my left side was hot and pulsating. I tried to get to sleep, but nothing was working. It was a long night. By the time morning came, my left side and neck were swollen. My father rushed me to the doctor, and the doctor rushed me to Wyckoff Hospital at Forest Hills in Queens, New York. They began to work on me as soon as I got there. My back wound wasn't bad, they said, but the wound on my left side was about five inches deep. They cut the stitches open, shoved a long narrow tube in my side wound, drained out all that dark bad blood, and then put me on intravenous drip. I felt so much better! They left the tube in me for the rest of the night. The doctor wrapped the wound up for a couple of days. It was healing great, so on the third day, he stitched me up again. I was feeling good and strong, and my family and friends came to see me every day.

At that time, I was seeing this cute little Irish girl named Delores. She had one cross-eye, which made her that much more adorable. She came up with a friend to visit me, and I'll never forget how she looked that day. I remember her long wavy blond hair and how it just smelled so clean. She had an impressive figure; she was wearing a bright royal blue skirt with mini pleats that just touched the top of her knees and a beautiful white on white blouse. She sat on the bed next to me, leaned down, gave me a big kiss, and said, "Can I love you?" I was feeling like I was in a dream. When my mother asked me "How come I've never met her? She is adorable," I changed the subject. In those days, I didn't want a steady girl, but my mother was right, she was adorable!

On the fourth day in the hospital, I had had enough. When the doctor came in to see me, I asked him if I could go home. He told me to give him one more day and when he did send me home I had to take it easy. "We don't want the inside stitches to open, so promise to take it easy." They sent me home the next day. I hung out in my basement for the next couple of weeks. I would listen to forty-five records. My friends and one of the girls that was with me that night of the fight, Cathy, would come over. She was also one of those beautiful Irish girls, with waist long blond hair and blue eyes. Every day, she would come over and take care of me. I respected her, she was only fourteen years old, much too young for me. I got better and went back to work, working out and hanging out on New Lots. I guess for a short while she was my guardian angel. I know what you're thinking; I like my Irish girls, my Italian girls, my Spanish girls, and so on.

I always appreciated God's gifts. Mr. Nero once told me that every day, I must work to keep the right attitude and that a man should not relinquish the action he is born to, even if it is flawed. When he came to the hospital to see me, he told me that I was a true Roman warrior; that made me so proud. I had once asked Mr. Nero why he was always in a good mood, and he said, "I manage my attitude." From that time on, I tried to manage my attitude and make him proud. After that war, the younger guys would call me Astro Boy (a cartoon superhero at that time).

New Lots Boys versus the Crescents

Six months went by since we had the wars with Hemlock and Sutter. I had become pretty good friends with most of the guys from Hemlock and Sutter and the Crescents, who were another gang that fought alongside Hemlock and Sutter.

One night, a few of my friends had gone to Crescent Street and gotten into a fight with a few of the Crescents, and they didn't fare so well. They had come back to New Lots to get our guys to go back and settle the score. I had just gotten home from work and had a big dinner. In those days, if I knew there was going to be trouble, I would eat very lightly or just suck on a piece of candy, but not that night; I had been a pig.

I got a call from Big Davy who told me what had happened. So I went to New Lots, and we all went back to Crescent Street. When we got there, the Crescents were waiting. They were good guys with lots of heart, and I liked them, Jerry G, Joe, and Tony. They were friendly nice guys, so don't ask me how, but the next thing I knew, I was fighting Jerry. My best asset is my ability to bang with two hands. I was fast and strong; he was just trying to protect himself. I didn't have the heart to hit him. I liked the guy, and he was just as strong as I was. We went at it till we couldn't breathe anymore, and it broke up; none of us were hurt. We all went back to New Lots Avenue. As I was walking back to New Lots, I threw up my steak and fries. That fight always bothered me, I knew these guys and I also knew my friends had started it. I hoped Jerry G forgave me a long time ago.

A good percentage of these guys we fucked up from Hemlock and Sutter, and the Crescents became today's wise guys. They became the inspiration for the movie *Goodfellas*, and together with the local politicians, they caused the moral breakdown of East New York. A lot of these guys remained friends of mine.

The only problem I did have was being blinded and naive to the worst kind of bad you can imagine,. At this young age, 1 learned short survival lessons like how to listen, watch, stay quiet, and stay back. I found I always knew when to act. I felt a kinship to every white gang in East New York. I walked through some of the most violent areas in East New York to get to the white strongholds. I always expected the worst on my journey. I stayed alert and aware, and I only relaxed when I got to my destination. Mr. Nero once told me if I want to keep a good attitude, value the people that make a good impact on your life.

The sun hardly shined on East New York; to me it was a great place to grow up. I saw the beauty, and it had been a great and rewarding experience.

New Lots Boys versus Cypress Hills Housing Project

The early 1950s shaped my life. The people from East New York taught me how to treat people. The people of East New York were generally happy; the men had their mostly blue-collar jobs, and the women were, for the most part, homemakers. You could go home for lunch, and your mother would be there for you.

I remember running home from school to watch my favorite television program, *American Bandstand*; at night and on weekends, I watched TV shows like *The Jackie Gleason Show*, *I Love Lucy*, *Dragnet*, *Flash Gordon*, *Have Gun Will Travel*, *Maverick*, *Captain Video*, *Roy Rogers*, *The Lone Ranger*, *Hopalong Cassidy*, and at night *The Million Dollar Movie*. Then there were the game shows, like *Beat the Clock*, *The $64,000 Question*, and *I Got a Secret*. On the weekends, nothing beats going to the Biltmore Theater and watching some of my favorite movies like *Shane*, *Blackboard Jungle*, *The Thing*, *Godzilla*, and *The Time Machine*.

There were street games I can't forget, like hide-and-seek, stoopball, skelly, Johnny on the pony, street hockey, hot beans, stick ball, and punchball and card games like war, go fish, or knuckles. In the summer, we would open the johnny pumps and put a milk crate under the water so it would shoot up in the air, and you could go under and cool yourself off.

There were two horse stables near where I lived, Rocking Horse and Henny Miller stables. They were south of Linden Boulevard. Much of the land was vacant, and they would put on Rodeo shows. I remember Papa Lang would come by on Saturday mornings with his horse and wagon that held about ten kids, and for ten cents, he would ride you around East New York for about an hour. There was a little man that stood on the back of the wagon so no one would fall off. He was always chewing and spitting; I thought he was chewing chocolate. I so looked forward to those rides. There would also be a small truck that would come around our block with a ride on it, like in an amusement park, or the vegetable wagon would also come down the block on Saturday mornings, and you could count on the Good Humor or the Bungalow Bar Ice Cream truck coming by your house every night in the summer months. How many of you remember the Charlotte Rouse man?

There was no air conditioning in those days, so everyone would hang outside to cool off. On Sunday mornings, I would go with my mother and brother to Blake Avenue to buy fruits and vegetables from the Jewish merchants who would buy fresh produce at the market and supply their push carts that would be lined up for blocks. Then we'd go to the fish market on the corner of Cleveland Street and Blake Avenue and then to the egg store.

Every vacant lot in East New York was utilized by an Italian immigrant to plant his fruits and vegetables, or the kids would play baseball or football in the vacant lots. I remember a vacant lot off Linden Boulevard between Linwood Street and Essex Street where every summer a carnival would set up rides, food, and games. The local churches would also have bazaars and feasts every year. In those days, you could take the subway, ride your bike, and walk anywhere and feel safe. My family moved from my aunt Fanny and uncle Jerry's house, where we rented the top floor apartment on Elton Street, between Linden Boulevard and Stanly Avenue, to a house my father bought one block south on Elton Street, between Stanly Avenue and Wortman Avenue.

That's when the first love of my life moved in with her family to the apartment where we used to live. She was a beautiful golden-haired angel. I fell in love for the very first time. She was seven, and I was eight. She didn't live there long before her family moved to Ozone Park, Queens, New York. It was about fifteen minutes away by car, but at that age, it might as well have been halfway around the world. Her name was Lillian, and my heart was broken for the first time in my little life. Those were magical years.

East New York's education system was second rate at best. Most teachers had their pet students to boost their own egos and neglected the rest of us. Maybe the times did not allow them to meet the challenges.

The 1960s gave birth to the hippies and the drug behavior. During the 1960s, drugs such as marijuana and LSD were easily accessible. The hippies rejected many of the society's morals and attitudes. Those magical times can be perceived as a thin veil behind which America's internal tensions were hidden, and we could not understand it's fear of an outside enemy, or maybe we did.

The historians believed that it was that roaring tide of young idealists that would change the country's perspective. The construction of most public housing like the Cypress Hills Housing Project created more crime, where half the population lived below the poverty line and received public assistance. They had no income or had very low income. Half of the male population had been arrested at one time or another. Poverty, crime, and drugs were the norm, with a large high school dropout rate. The whole idea was a social economic political folly, when all the system had to do was to create jobs and small businesses in the area. The honest people that lived in the Cypress Hills projects were just swept into the abyss along with the rest of East New York.

It was another one of those great summer nights. I finished work, went home, took a shower, ate, and got dressed in my fight gear: a pair of loose cotton black chino pants, a white T-shirt, and a pair of tan desert boots. I was feeling good and on my way to New Lots Avenue, and I knew my friends would be at the Triangle. Like I said, it was a great night. There were about fifty guys hanging out: the older guys, my friends, and the younger guys. I had an itch that I had to get scratched, so I asked if anyone wanted to take a walk to Hemlock and Sutter; it was just about as Far East in Brooklyn as you could get, on the border of Queens, New York. The guys from Hemlock and Sutter along with the guys from Crescent Street were nice guys with pretty young ladies. It was mostly an Italian neighborhood. We had our little wars, but for the most part, they were good allies. No one wanted to take a walk. That's when I heard this funny and slow laugh, and out popped this red-headed pug-nosed guy named Sandy Mick, Mick is a term of endearment for a cool Irish dude with this big ass smile. There weren't many Irish guys on New Lots Avenue, but every Irish guy I knew was tough and had heart. Out walked Sandy, as bad as they came, drunk or sober, you knew he was right there. I don't know if I had ever seen him sober. Maybe on this particular night that was a good thing. Now I don't know if I already told you, but I didn't drink, smoke, or do drugs. My vices were simple; just read on. So Sandy and I headed east down New Lots Avenue. The only safe way to get to Hemlock and Sutter was to walk around the Cypress Hills Housing Project. New Lots Avenue ended at Fountain Avenue, directly in the middle of Cypress Hills Projects. If you made a right, you could walk to Linden Boulevard and around the projects; and if you made a left, you could walk to Sutter Avenue and around the north end of the projects. Even Sandy was sober enough to know that this wasn't a very good idea. I had to say it, and those two little words said it all, "Follow me." Again with that laugh, he said "Let's go!" We started across Fountain Avenue into the middle of the projects. Sandy looked at me and said, "Do we know what the fuck we're doing?" I said, "Trust me. Just do what I do." Like I said, it was a nice summer night, not the best time to be trying to pull this off. In the middle of the projects, there were benches where you could sit out on a nice night like tonight, and wouldn't you know, there were dozens of young bros hanging out all over the center of the projects. We just kept walking like we belonged. When we got to the middle of the projects, everyone was just looking at us like we were from Mars. We just kept moving. Everyone stopped what they were doing and were now looking at our two pale faces. By this time, we were three-quarters of the way through the projects. The bros were now behind us in a large group and walking toward us. I turned and was now slowly walking backward and looking straight at them. The lead bro said, "What the fuck are you white motherfuckers doing here?" I looked straight in his face and said, "New Lots, motherfuckers." They came right at us. I told Sandy again to follow me, and we turned and ran through the projects across Euclid Avenue. When we got across Euclid Avenue and out of the project, I told Sandy to grab one of those metal garbage cans. The homes on the east side of the project were mostly two-story brick houses with small front yards, with a couple of garbage cans in each yard. We each picked up one metal garbage can and ran back across Euclid Avenue, swinging and cracking heads as they turned, and ran back into the project, tripping over each other. We ran into the project, threw the cans down, and ran back out to get two more cans. After three or four times, we were done. We dropped more than a few bros and split east to Crescent Street with the bros still in hot pursuit. The bros ran one block to Crescent Street, stopped, turned, and went back to the project. They knew better than to venture into this well-equipped Italian stronghold. When we got to Hemlock and Sutter, Sandy looked at me and said, "What the fuck was that?" Needless to say, we didn't walk back the same way.

In my early days with the New Lots Boys, every Sunday, Sandy would go to St. Gabriel Church. I, on the other hand, only went on Christmas and Easter. One Sunday, Sandy was coming out of church and saw me standing outside in front of the church and asked, "Q, were you in church?" I said no, and he said, "So what are you doing here?" I said, "All the beautiful girls are at church on Sunday morning, and I just might get to walk one of those honeys home." He looked at me and said, "I have to go to church. I'm a bad guy. You don't do shit wrong but fight and work, so why would you have to go to church?" It made sense to me.

That day, I met Carol D, one of the most beautiful Italian girls in the neighborhood and one of the sweetest girls I knew. I walked her home and asked her out to a movie. The next weekend, I took her to the Kanima movie theater on Pitkin Avenue to see *Teacher's Pet* with Doris Day and Clark Gable. After the movie, on the way home, she told me one of the older guys in the neighborhood, Scotty, had asked her out that week and she had said yes. Out of respect, I didn't ask her out again, but I always thought about her; she was very sweet. Scotty was two or three years older than I was. I was fourteen years old at that time, and a two—or three-year difference made a big deal when it came to the streets.

One day, while we were hanging out in the park, Sally V told me that Scotty was one bad dude; he looked like it, and I didn't question it. One week later, I was walking east on New Lots Avenue and Essex Street with nine of my crew, the young New Lots Boys. In the opposite direction, three of the older guys, Ira S, Ronnie G, and Scotty, were walking toward us. When they got up to us, Ira said, "How about us three wipe the street with you nine and not break a sweat?" I said, "I don't think so." We went at it, three on one. It took us about half a minute to drop the three of them. I said, "How about our top three here tonight fight you three?" It was me, JR, and Mike R. Scotty said, "I want you, punk!" Now Scotty did look bad; dressed all in black, with his collar up, dark brown eyes that showed indifference, and the deep emphasis in his voice. I have to say, I was a little apprehensive and I had a desire not to move. I had already been through a few gang wars with the Liberty Park guys. We would go to Liberty Park with sometimes fifty to one hundred of our guys. I had been working out with Mr. Nero for two years, and at that time, I rode my heavy butcher bike with a large basket in the front. Every day after school, I would ride that bike for miles; that was most of my road work. So we went at it. Ira dropped JR, Ronnie G dropped Mike R, and I dropped Scotty on to the sidewalk. He jumped up, looked at me, and with a break in this intense voice said, "Your days are numbered, motherfucker!" Next thing, they were just three black silhouettes in the distance.

I lived on Elton Street, two blocks south of Linden Boulevard. The area of East New York I lived in had very few homes; it mostly consisted of light industrial factories and minimum-wage jobs, and because of the 25 percent unemployment rate in Puerto Rico at that time, New York now had its new low-wage immigrants, who were happy to have a job and for probably less than the minimum wage. I was in grade school, and every morning when I went to school, men and woman were going to work; and every night, they would go home to their families. Some of the older Puerto Rican guys would open small grocery stores, and the younger guys would work on the push carts on Blake Avenue. For the most part, they were very friendly people; and like all immigrants, we all had our dirt bags. Still, we younger guys had a problem; I believe it was more of a macho turf thing. I remember hearing that this old

Puerto Rican woman, who had an apartment on Blake Avenue, had a statue of St. Mary, and that the statue was crying tears of blood. That night, all of the Italian and Irish boys and girls had to go and see it. There was a line around the block, with New Lots Boys. Puerto Rican gangs like the El Tones were also there. I would like to think out of respect for this miracle there were no problems that night. (I've heard that certain species of fish will grow according to the size of their environment. Put them in a smaller aquarium, and they remain small even at adulthood. Release them into a large body of water, and they grow to their intended size. People are similar. If they live in a harsh and limiting environment, they stay small. But put them someplace that encourages growth, and they will expand to reach their potential.)

EAST NEW YORK VERSUS THE BATTLE OF MAX THE MAYORS

The Ambassador of East New York, Mr. Steven S, alias Hi Ho, stood five feet ten, weighed one hundred and fifty pounds, and had a slight muscular build and thick brown curly hair.

One hot August night of 1962, Hi Ho and a few of the crew were hanging out on New Lots Avenue, around 1:00 a.m. Not much was happening, mostly talking and trying to figure what to do for tonight, when a car pulled up to the guys and Stevie S got out all beaten up. He told the guys he was at this bar in Flatbush called Max the Mayors. It was known to be a great place to pick up chicks and also had a violent reputation.

Besides the usual crew that hung out there, there were also a dozen of these huge bouncers inside the bar, posing like bad asses, looking to fuck with people. When a few guys would have a problem, and if you got into a fight, the odds were very much against you. Most of the guys from East New York had been going there all summer. I had never been there, and much to my surprise, I never heard of any incident. Now that was very unusual for any of the crews from East New York, but let's not forget the summer isn't over.

Stevie S had gone there by himself, thinking maybe a few of the guys might be there; none of our crew was there, so he asked this cute girl to dance. Stevie had that classic southern Italian look, handsome, five feet nine, slim build, and had an olive complexion, dark wavy hair, and dark brown eyes. Stevie was dancing when some guy came up to him, cut in, and told him the girl was his girlfriend. The girl denies that she is this guy's girl, and as Stevie continues to dance, this dude punches Stevie in the back of the head.

Stevie turned and started fighting with this dude when his friends jumped in; the bouncers broke it up and forced Stevie and these guys to take it outside the bar. Considering all that happened, it was a miracle that Stevie could get back in his car and drive home. When Stevie told Hi Ho and the guys what happened, Hi Ho and our guys immediately started to round up guys to avenge Stevie. Our guys got a hold of Fat Patsy from the old mill crew. He took our guys in his car and drove all over East New York looking for all the violent street gangs we had allied with to go back to Max the Mayors and deal a devastating first blow.

After about an hour, they were able to round up around thirty guys; this was a drop in the bucket for the job that needed to be done. Hi Ho told everyone to go home and to meet up again Saturday night at White Castle on Atlantic Avenue and Berriman Street. White Castle was a central place in East New York and a popular place for white gang members to meet.

By this time, I had been a New Lots boy for a few years. There were the older guys, the younger guys, and our crew, which was in the middle. By now, we all had integrated like a small army; everyone in East New York had at one time or another seen us in action. You wouldn't dare come to our neighborhood without an invitation, but we would come to yours anytime we felt like it. We also made house calls.

No one fucked with us; we had that do or die mentality, and if you did get the balls to fuck with us, you'd earned the art of war the hard way. Even the wise guys backpedaled when it came to dealing with us on the street; man to man, they didn't stand a chance. During the week leading up to the battle of Max the Mayors, Hi Ho the ambassador went to every street corner in East New York, recruiting some of the worst street criminals, East New York's finest.

Hi Ho told everyone what was going down and gave instructions where to meet: 8:00 p.m. at White Castle, be armed and wear a white bandana around your heads to show you are from East New York. I'm not sure when exactly the New Lots Boys got started. Some of the old timers in the neighborhood told us they think it was started sometime in the 1930s the Mafia and Murder Incorporated would come to our corner to pay their respects and do business. The organized gangs of that time would dump their victim's bodies in the old mill swamp areas of East New York. Till this day, there is a mosaic tile plaque cemented in the ground at the small triangle where Livonia Avenue intersects with New Lots Avenue that say's "New Lots Boys 1942"; it was a tribute to the guys on the corner that went off to fight in World War II.

Hi Ho told me that he was a young man when he first heard about the New Lots Boys and started to see them around the neighborhood. He heard that they were a bad ass street gang, and people were terrified of them. Hi Ho and his brother would go with their mother to take the IRT train downtown Brooklyn clothes shopping, and they would have to pass the Triangle where the New Lots Boys hung out. They were one tough-looking crew. Hi Ho knew at that very young age he wanted and needed to be a New Lots boy.

You have to understand what a violent neighborhood this was, and all the guys that were to join us consider it to be a great East New York social event, the equivalent of a debutante ball in Westchester New York. To all these psychopaths, criminals, and violence-loving maniacs, this was going to be a night of fun. None of these guys gave a shit about avenging Stevie. It was the idea of going to a bar and kicking ass that made this night so appealing. Most of these guys thought being allied with the New Lots Boys wasn't such a bad idea. A few of these guys wound up in the Goodfellas crew you saw in the movies.

Saturday night came. Hi Ho and the New Lots Boys drove to White Castle. There were hundreds of guys hanging around. Both sides of Atlantic Avenue were filled with cars that will be taking us to Flatbush. Till this day, Hi Ho said he has no idea how many guys we actually had. He heard anywhere from 200 and as much as 500. I'll never know for sure. All he knew was that we had enough warriors to invade a small country. Hi Ho told everybody how to get to our destination in case they get separated from the caravan we'll be riding in. He also told everyone to park in the back of the parking lot with their cars turned around so we can make a fast getaway.

Hi Ho's plan was simple. Hi Ho, Stevie, and a few of our guys would go in. Stevie would point out the dudes that fucked him up and tell them to come outside. There might be fifty guys plus the bouncers. Once they came outside, they would be greeted by a wall of mad men with bats, pipes, and other blunt weapons, and they would have no idea of what they were in for. That was Hi Ho's plan. Here is what happened. We pulled into the parking lot. We parked in the back with the cars turned around. Everybody puts on a white bandana made from sheets or towels. Everyone gets out the weapons of their choice. Hi Ho is standing next to Babe Costanza and Anthony Stabile, two extremely violent young lads. Both have car antennas, and Babe also has a dagger. Babe is about five feet eleven, with light hair with movie star looks. He was the leader of Liberty Park Crew, a bad ass that lived for nights like this.

Out of nowhere, these two drunks walked up to Hi Ho and demanded to know what the fuck we were doing here. (You, the reader, how many times where you drunk enough to have walked up to hundreds of armed, violent-looking young men?) They got their answer immediately. Babe and Anthony started whipping the shit out of them with car antennas. It was a warm night, and they were dressed in T-shirts that were originally white and were now red with blood as were their heads and faces. These two idiots sobered up immediately and were now running for their lives. Babe and Anthony chased them right into Max the Mayors. Hi Ho and our crew followed Babe and Anthony in so they don't get attacked by the bouncers.

When you entered the bar, you first had to walk through this long narrow corridor. In the front entry was a bouncer who looked like a wrestler. He sat on a folding chair with two legs off the floor and leaning against the wall. If he suspected that you were underage, which at that time was eighteen years, he would check your proof, like a driver's license or a draft card. As these two bloody dudes ran into the club, the bouncer noticed that most of the guys chasing them were underage. He told this crew to stop and demanded proof of age. Then Red Bear came with his trademark doubled up washing machine hose and yelled, "Here's my proof!" and cracked the bouncer over the head. The two chair legs slid out from under him, and down he went. The guys that came in behind Red Bear kicked and cracked the bouncer. Now all the guys from East New York go storming in.

Here's a little word about Red Bear. At fourteen years old, he was five feet ten and weighed one hundred and seventy pounds. He was totally fearless and a bit insane. He had picked up this hose in the street; whenever he hit someone with it, he would put a notch in it. This included drive-bys, cracking people in the ass. He had more notches on that hose than Bill the Kid and Wyatt Earp put together. He was Hi Ho's all-time favorite human being, and I loved Bear's spirit.

The first thing Hi Ho saw when he entered the bar area was Ralphie F and his brother Hank attacking the band. These poor musicians never knew what hit them. When Hi Ho told the guys that anyone without a bandana was a legitimate target, he meant the people that came outside to fight. They took Hi Ho at his word and fucked up anyone without a bandanna. Now there was around sixty of our crew inside. The place was packed as usual, and most had no clue of what's going on or the nightmare about to happen.

In the middle of all this pandemonium, Hi Ho heard one particularly loud scream. It was coming from behind the bar, Hi Ho looked up and saw Red Bear behind the bar beating the bartender with his hose. Hi Ho asked Bear why he's hitting the bartender. The answer was obvious; he's not wearing a bandana. By now, everyone in the place was aware of what's happening. People were terrified; the bouncers don't know what to do. The head bouncer who everyone feared was one big dude with a southern accent called the Rebel. He was reputed to have been a professional heavyweight boxer. He stood there chomping on a cigar butt and was in a state of shock when someone yelled out "What's going on, Rebel?" Rebel has no idea; all he saw were dozens of guys rushing in and cracking everyone in sight, even the girls. This crew were taking no prisoners. One of our guys cracks the Rebel over the head with a bat. Hi Ho saw the rebel went down then heard Babe yell out "Gimme the shotgun!" By now, we had established credibility. No one doubted that this sick pack of animals would shoot the place up.

Now there was total terror in the air. There were now guys fighting with girls for a spot under the tables when the shotgun went off. In the middle of all this, Hi Ho was laughing his balls off, between beating the band, the bartender, and now the threat of a shotgun in a packed bar. Stevie spotted the guys that beat him up. They told these guys to go outside; they agreed, not that they had a choice. They had no idea that all they saw so far was the tip of the iceberg. We went outside, and the Max the Mayors crew and the bouncers followed us.

As soon as they came out, they met a couple of hundred bats and pipes. Within seconds, the Max the Mayors crew and bouncers were laid out all over the parking lot, which was now painted red with blood. People inside the bar were now coming out to watch the show in the parking lot; the guys that were still standing in the parking lot were now trying desperately to get back in the bar. One of our guys, Divo, runs back in when he saw the Rebel and started whipping him with a car antenna. Divo was Italian, tall and handsome, one of the toughest guys in East New York and one of the very few with a good mind. You just knew he would have a good future, that's only if he got out of East New York. All the guys from East New York were now trying to get back in the bar now that they had a taste of blood. Attila the Hun would have been embarrassed to have this crew; even his warriors weren't this violent.

Now our guys were furious that there was nobody else to beat up. So they start smashing every car window in the parking lot. There were bodies all over the parking lot, and we did not know if anyone was dead, which was a real possibility. Hi Ho told our guys it's time to go before the cops get here. One of our guys, Mousey, has a pipe and began smashing the big neon sign that says "Max the Mayors." The East New York crew wasn't quite done yet.

Our guys finally had enough. They ran to the back parking lot and got in their cars, stepping over bodies along the way. Hi Ho was driving with Barry, one of the best get away drivers in East New York. He had a Pontiac Bonneville. He drove that car 125 mph all the way back to New Lots Avenue; this half hour ride took about ten minutes. Hi Ho said that ride was scarier than the fight. All the New Lots Boys started checking in; everybody was in a great mood after such an invigorating event. Then they realized Frenchie and Anthony weren't back. A half an hour later, Anthony's brother, Tommy, and his Uncle Tom came to the corner with our friend Ira. They told us that Frenchie and Anthony got caught by the cops and were at the police station. They asked what happened. They said not to worry and it will get

Richard G Quarantello

taken care of. The owner and the bouncers went to the police station to press charges. The bouncers wanted to kill Frenchie and Anthony.

When the owner of Max the Mayor hears Anthony's last name, he asked if he had a relative named Tom, referring to Anthony's uncle. When Anthony said yes, he was told to contact him and get him down to the station, that's why they came down to the corner to get the story. Uncle Tom talked to the owner of Max the Mayors, who then told the cops he's dropping the chargers and that they got the wrong guys.

The cops and the bouncers were furious, but the owner was adamant about it. As it turned out, the owner was paying protection to Uncle Tom. Obviously, he didn't get his money's worth. Nobody was killed that night, which was very hard to believe. No one from East New York got as much as a scratch. A month after that incident, Max the Mayors was burnt to the ground. The owner got the insurance money. Anthony and his family went on with the mob life. Anthony was mentioned several times in the movie *Goodfellas*. As for all the East New York hoodlums who took part in this atrocity, "a good time was had by one and all."

New Lots Boys versus Car Dudes

It was the winter of 1963, one of those frigid bone-chilling days. It was snowing all day. I just got home. It was a Friday night with over two feet of snow on the ground. The wind was howling, and by the time I got home from work, there were four and five-foot snowdrifts covering all the parked cars. There was an empty space where a car must have just pulled out in front of my house. I pulled in, locked the doors, and made a beeline for my warm, comfortable house. My intention all day was to come home and take a hot shower. Fish was the Catholic Friday night cuisine. So I took my hot shower, put on a pair of gray sweat pants, a sweatshirt, and a pair of thick white cotton socks, had dinner, and just sat down to watch some TV. I had no intentions of going out into this hawk again. It was a shit day all day; I had a carpet job in Harlem on Edgecombe Avenue at the Edgecombe Hotel. My helper Willie who is black and I the only white dude for blocks around. I worked in Harlem when there was a carpet job to be done, mostly because none of the other white guys in the shop wanted to; not once did I have a problem. I found out that the Edgecombe Hotel was a place where bros would take prostitutes or their *gumadas* (Italian for girlfriend). The hotel was an old red brick building that stood alone. When you walked into the lobby, you'll immediately feel you were walking into the nineteenth century, with this strong pungent mildew smell that the panel walls, wool carpet, and the dry red-and-black velvet wall paper peeling off the walls in almost every corner had absorbed from years of people smoking and the damp New York winter. With its beautifully paneled tin ceiling, you feel like you were in an Old World New York hotel. We were there for three days, and as soon as we finished installing the carpet, cleaning up, and putting back one bed and one dresser and walked out the door, a couple would pass us and walk in. This went on all day. Some of the ladies were sexy and pretty; for most of them, you would need at least a few shoots of tequila and a brown paper bag, or you must have been in jail for at least five years. It was my last day working at the Edgecombe Hotel. We finished up, packed our tools, and headed for the entry to the hotel when the bro at the front desk said for twenty dollars apiece, he could get us laid or have a blow job. We started to laugh. First, we only had five dollars between us; second, there wasn't enough tequila in the state of New York. Willie told the guy he would rather fuck bigfoot's mother. We made a beeline for the car; I started it up and turned up the heat. I had a 1951 Ford that my father gave me for five hundred dollars, which he put on a 1955 Ford. It was my first car, a standard shift with three on the column, and the heater was great and well appreciated.

I just sat down to relax when the phone rang. I ran to pick it up. To tell you the truth, I was warm and bored. It was Joey Jet, one of our original New Lots crew. He was next door to my house, at my aunt Day Day and Uncle Frankie. Jet was going out with my cousin Marie, one of the cutest young ladies around. Marie and her brother Frankie were like my sister and brother. Marie was sick with the flu, and the Jet like me was bored and wanted to know what my plans were for tonight. I told him my plans were to not go out into this shit. He told me that most of the guys and girls are going to the Biltmore Theater. The Biltmore Theater was on the corner of New Lots and Miller Avenue. I said you drive; he said OK. I got dressed and run out, and Jet was already in his car. I jumped into the car, and we were off. The movie playing at the Biltmore Theater was *It's a Mad, Mad, Mad, Mad World*, a great comedy that year. Now I'm in the mood. We drove north, up Elton Street, to New Lots Avenue and made a left turn about a half mile to Miller Avenue. You can see the lights of the theater a few blocks away, and they looked warm and inviting. When we got to Miller Avenue, we made a left turn trying to look for a parking spot. For the next hour, we drove up and down every block in a five block radius. This was going to be our last try; we had already decided to go to the Galaxy Diner for hot chocolate and apple pie, and on this cold night that sounded good. We started to head down Miller Avenue again. We were about twenty feet to the end of the block when this dude came around the corner, headed up Miller Avenue, and stopped about four feet from the front of Jets car. Miller Avenue at that time was a two-way street, with the snow still coming down and the snowdrifts that covered the cars on both sides of the Street leaving a narrow path where only one car was lucky to get through. This guy was now right in front of us blocking our way; there were cars behind us all the way back to New Lots Avenue. Jet rolled down his window, waved his hand, and asked this dude to back up. All the windows on this guy's car came down, and the guys in the car told us to back the fuck up; they were laughing and fucking with us. Jet said, "Just back the car up." This one dude, the driver of the car, jumped out, horns were still honking behind us. I stepped out of our car once again, not getting blindsided sitting in the passenger seat, and told this dude to back his fuckin' car out. I saw the other three dudes getting out of the car. This motherfucker was now walking toward me with his hands up boxing style, my first sign that this shit head can't throw a punch. I stepped out, closed my car door, and walked right up to this idiot, telling him at the same time to get back in his car, that was only until I had my punching distance. I hit him with a quick overhand right. This moron went down, hit the back of his head with the bumper of his car, and went to sleep on the compacted snow. Jet jumped out, and this idiot's friends were already out. They stopped dead in their tracks when they saw their friend hit the floor. I told these guys to pick up their friend and back out this piece of shit car. They couldn't get out of there fast enough. There were guys in the street that got out of their cars that were stuck behind me. They shook my hand, and one guy said that he'd never seen a guy get hit so quickly and go down so fuckin' fast. I said thanks guys, and we were off to the Galaxy Diner. We got to the diner, and a few of my other friends were already there. They couldn't get in the movie either. I ordered hot chocolate and apple pie and treated myself to two scoops of ice cream on top of my apple pie. Did that just make your mouth water? This wasn't the kind of night to hang out. I told Jet to take me home. Consumer Carpets called and told my mother that there was no work tomorrow; all the jobs were canceled. It was still snowing by the time I got home. It was early enough, so I called my girlfriend Patty, the prettiest person I knew inside and out. She lived in South Brooklyn, and I told her I had no work tomorrow. So the next day, I walked to the New Lots Avenue Train station and got off at the Nevins Street station downtown Brooklyn and walked a few blocks. She lived at 21 Douglas Street. I had very little resistance for her type of beauty. She had an Italian mother and an Irish father. My mother always told me Italian and Irish couples make the best-looking children, and she was living proof. This is one young lady that will always be in my heart.

New Lots Boys versus Club Chateau

Junior had just come home from Korea. He was the first one of my friends to join the army. It was 1963, before the Vietnam War. He was on a two-week leave and looking to have a good time, so JR, his brother Frankie, and I went to meet a friend of mine, Nina, and two of her girlfriends. We met the girls on the corner of Blake and Atkins Avenues. This was going to be a great night to hang out.

The three girls were as cute as they could be. A warm summer Saturday night and cute girls, what could go wrong? We were just hanging and talking when three bros walked by, staring at the girls like we were invisible. (To me, when a guy was with a girl, no matter how hot she was, it was off limits, out of respect for the guy. If you said hello, you eyeballed the guy, whether you knew him or not, black or white, it didn't matter.) They kept staring even as they passed us. I wanted to say something but I didn't say a thing. JR was home on leave, and I didn't want him to get into any trouble; I wanted him to have a good time that night and not have to worry.

So as they walked by, one bro had to open his big mouth. He was still staring at the girls when he said, "Hey, girls, what ya doin' with dose honky motherfuckers?" I didn't even know what a honky was at that time, but I did know what a motherfucker was. That's when they stopped and stared at us, and that's when I turned and looked at JR and Frankie and said, "Sorry, but the shit's on." So I pulled a Big Davy; I walked right up to the one with the big mouth, with my right hand stretched out like I was going to shake the big mouth's hand and said, "What's up?" They were pointing at us and laughing. He put out his hand, and I threw him a quick overhand right, knocking him out. The other two bros turned and ran. JR and Frankie ran after one bro, and I chased the other bro south on Atkins Avenue. I caught up to him halfway down the block, threw him up against a parked car, and began to punch the shit out of him; he was crying like a baby.

The guy that JR and Frankie ran after got away, so they ran over to where I was. I told them to hold his arms, and they did, and I began to load up on this piece of shit. JR and Frankie both said, "You're going to kill him!" but to me, it was a lesson I was teaching; you can't disrespect every white boy because there just might be a price to pay. When it was over, we went back to where the girls were. They were gone, so we decided to go to the Triangle.

The week before, a few of us had gone to a club in Ridgewood, Brooklyn. Foxy and I were invited by two girls we had met from Hemlock and Sutter. This part of Ridgewood was an Italian stronghold, with pretty tough crews that hung out in local bars and private clubs. This was a neighborhood we weren't very familiar with. I don't know how we managed to find this place, but we did.

We knew enough to park our cars on the side street in case there was a problem. When we turned the corner onto Wyckoff Avenue, there were all kinds of boys and girls hanging outside the club. When we got to the entrance, the club was packed wall to wall. The club Chateau was an old store with the entrance in the middle and two blacked out picture windows on the left and the right sides of the door. A few of us walked into the club, and a few of the guys hung outside. We had a great night. The guy that ran the place invited us back again. I said, "Thanks, man. We had a great time."

When Frankie, JR, and I got to the Triangle, Hi Ho said, "Hey, Q, let's go to the club we went to last week." I said, "Cool, let's do it." A few of the other guys hanging out on the corner asked where we were going. Hi Ho said, "To this great club we went to last week." Twenty-two of us jumped into three cars, and we were off. I told JR, "This can't be good. It might not be a good idea for you to go." He said, "Hey, man, I'm looking to have a good time tonight. Let's go!" It took about forty minutes to get there. Again, we parked our cars on the side street and walked to the Club. We had three cars and parked them in different spots so it didn't look like there were so many of us. That was a good idea! Like the week before, the place was packed, inside and out. Some of us went inside, and a few guys stayed outside. When you walked into the club, the bar was straight ahead, about twenty feet in length. There was a juke box on the right side, close to the front. From the juke box to the bar, they had a bench attached to the wall that people could sit on. On the left, next to the wall, there was a long bench almost to the bar. It was fixed up really cool, with wooden floors and those old tin ceilings, kind of an old western bar with a full-length mirror in back of the bar. There were some of the prettiest girls I've ever seen. I walked up to the bar and ordered a 7-Up with a twist. There was a cute little Italian girl standing next to me. I remember her because she had dark brown hair with hazel eyes and freckles. I was in love! I paid for her drink, and she and I talked. She had come with two of her girlfriends. They were neighborhood girls. Her two girlfriends walked over to us, also good-looking young ladies. I was kind of shy at that time, and I was just trying to think of a way to get this girl's number and still keep my cool when before I could get the words out of my mouth I heard "Q! There is a problem! Foxy just walked outside with some guy!" Apparently, Foxy was dancing with a young lady when this guy walked up to him and said, "Yo, dude, I want to dance with her." Foxy tried to be polite and said, "OK, when the song is over." But the guy said, "No, I want to dance with her now!" Foxy looked at this piece of shit and said "Go fuck yourself!" This guy started to walk outside then turned and looked at Foxy and said, "Hey, scumbag, you! Outside, motherfucker!" Foxy excused himself and went outside. Half the guys in the place headed outside behind Foxy. Hi Ho, a few of our guys that were in the club, and I walked outside to see what was up. Before I got outside the door, I could see a few of our guys that were outside were already at war. I ran outside throwing punches. It was 1963; I was eighteen years old. I didn't drink or smoke, was still working out at least five days a week, and was work strong; everyone I hit went down. I was feeling great when I got kicked in the head by this guy standing on top of a car. I turned, grabbed this guy, and threw him off the car. I was ready to crack him and then I saw it was Lee. I said, "What the fuck are you doing?" He said, "Sorry, Q," and we returned to the battlefield. More and more guys were coming, from neighborhood bars and other clubs. We had twenty-two of our guys, but there were at least fifty to seventy-five Ridgewood guys, and we were fucked. We hung firm! There where Ridgewood guys laid out all over the street. As I was banging, I saw our guys now across the street. They were carrying someone. I ran across the street; the fight had stopped for a minute. I said, "What happened?" And they said, "JR got hit with a baseball bat in the chest." I looked at JR, and he was having a hard time breathing. I looked across the street, and there were at least fifty guys standing in front of the Club. I was pissed!

I ran across the street into these guys banging. All our guys were right behind me. It was conquer or die! I saw one guy run past me. Ralphie B was a few feet away from me. This poor bastard got hit with a right hand; I don't think I have ever seen anyone get hit so hard. Ralphie's nickname was one punch Ralph, now you know why. I picked up a metal garbage can and ran into the club swinging. I hit a couple of guys then cracked the jukebox, turned, and threw the metal garbage can at the mirror behind the bar. I saw Foxy throw a metal garbage can through one of the storefront windows. I picked up the garbage can and threw it through the other window. Girls were screaming; guys were laid out all over. I ran out of the club still banging. I don't remember being tired or out of breath; my adrenalin was pumping. I ran back out the front door.

Outside was packed with guys I didn't recognize now. I ran out of the club throwing punches. I hit this one big dude; he hardly moved. I grabbed him by his jacket, spun him around with my left hand to keep him off balance, and threw at least a dozen straight right hands. He fell against a parked car. As I was still right handing him, this other dude cracked me over my head with a bottle. I turned to grab him, and he ran. One of our guys, Snail, was a couple of feet from me. As the guy ran in his direction, I yelled out to Snail to grab that motherfucker. Snail grabbed him! I ran and got a hold of the guy and ran this fat fuck through the store window next to the club. I had blood running down my head and back. I was pissed! I picked up a bat that was lying in the street. It looked like a war zone! There was yelling and screaming, and all I could see and hear were cop cars all over. I cracked a couple more guys, and everyone seemed to back off. Everyone was running, and I didn't see any of our guys, so I headed down a side street. Cop cars were coming from every direction. I didn't know where I was going. Now my adrenalin was pumping blood from my head.

I had on a white summer jacket. I took off my jacket and applied pressure to my head wound. I had a white T-shirt on, and it was also soaked with blood. I was thinking, "How the fuck am I going to get home like this?" when I heard "Hey, Q!" It was Ralphie B driving up the block. His car was packed with our guys. I squeezed in, and we headed back to the neighborhood. JR was in one of the other cars. I told Ralphie to go to JR's house. I wanted to see how he was doing. When we got there, he was standing outside, a little fucked up but OK. I was coming down now from my adrenalin high, and the bleeding had stopped. I asked JR if he had a clean T-shirt I could borrow. I washed up and put on the clean T-shirt, and we headed for the corner.

We all had our own war stories that evening. Hi Ho told me that he had seen the guy with the bat that hit JR. The guy had run and jumped into a taxi cab, and they drove off. Hi Ho said, "I wonder if he knew how lucky he was; he owes that cab driver his life." Hi Ho said he saw Foxy wrestling with this guy on the ground and that the guy had a knife in his hand. All he knew was there were guys fighting and laid out all over the street and cops were all around. Hi Ho picked up a car antenna and whacked the guy fighting with Foxy across the head. He felt something hit him across his back, turned to crack him with the antenna, and it was a cop. He dropped the antenna, and the cop threw him against a wall. Foxy cracked the guy he was fighting a couple of more times. Two other cops grabbed Foxy and the other guy and put them up against the wall with a few other Ridgewood guys. The guy Foxy was fighting with was all fucked up and told the cops he wanted to press charges against Hi Ho and Foxy. Hi Ho told the cop that this scumbag tried to stab Foxy with a knife. They looked down at the sidewalk; there were bats, pipes, bottles, car antennas, and a couple of knives. Hi Ho told Foxy, "As soon as the cops turn away, let's split." They went to turn and run when Hi Ho got cracked in the back by the same cop. The cop pointed his gun at Hi Ho's head and said, "If you try to run again, I'll shoot you in the fucking head!" One of the cops asked Hi Ho and Foxy, "Where are you guys from?" Before they could answer, a bunch of Ridgewood guys yelled out, "They're from New Lots!" Hi Ho told the cop, "We don't live anywhere near New Lots." A black cop walked up to them, which was pretty rare in those days, and told Hi Ho and Foxy to get the fuck out of there. Hi Ho thought to himself, "There are guys lying all over the street, and it looks like there are a hundred guys just looking to kill me and Foxy." Then they heard someone whistle. It was Ralphie, so they ran and got into the car. Then they picked me up, and that's when we went to JR's house. Ridgewood, Brooklyn, at that time was a small town with honest, hardworking family people. Ridgewood, like East New York, inherited the new infected society. The powers that be have only one interest: their own. There were no heroes to get the incompetent monarchy out of our way.

New Lots Boys versus Bullies Revenge

It was the summer of 1963. That year, I changed jobs from working for Consumer Carpets to a good friend of mine, Bankie. He opened his own carpet installation business. By 1963, I was a carpet mechanic and would go out on my own with a helper. At Consumer Carpets, I worked with the only black guy, there Bonnie, so I guess Bankie thought it would be OK to hook me up with one of two black dudes that work in his shop. I worked with Eugene for almost two years, a really cool guy. He was very surprised to hear me singing songs by the likes of King Pleasure, Arthur Prysock, Lambert, Hendricks, and Ross or Oscar Brown Jr. We would sing in the car every day. Eugene turned me on to Billy Holiday and Dinah Washington. He said he never heard a white dude singing or even knowing who these people where. I told Eugene there are only a few things I like to do, and that's work, working out, music, and the appreciation of a fine young lady and how they made me feel, the softness of their lips, the clean smell of their hair or just being near me, and a touch. Oh yeah, knocking out some scumbag felt pretty good to.

This one day, I had Bankie's car, a 1954 big old rust-colored Pontiac. I dropped Eugene at the train station. He lived somewhere near Jamaica, Queens, New York. I took the car back to Bankie's house on Norwood Street off Atlantic Avenue and jogged home about two miles. I was in great shape and again testing myself by running home through the worst area East New York had to offer. I stopped by the Triangle to see if any of my friends were hanging out. A few of our guys were there, Big Davy, Sonny, and a few of our crew. I wanted to know what the plan was for tonight. It was simple. Big Davy said if we can get a ride, we thought we would go to the Bow Wow. The Bow Wow was a Nathans-type restaurant with foot-long hot dogs, hamburgers, roast beef sandwiches on a bun, and great French fries. It was on Cross Bay Boulevard and 163 Avenue in Howard Beach, around three or four miles from the Triangle. I was sweating from the run, so I told the guys I'm going home to take a shower and I'll try to get my brother's car and come right back. So off I went.

My brother had a new 1962 gold Chevy Impala. He was in the army reserves and had to spend six months away. At that time, he left his car home. I paid the payments on the car for those six months, but I still wasn't allowed to use the car. I took a shower and got dressed, naturally in my fight gear, while listening to my mother yell at me from the time I got into the house till I left. Where are you going, I made supper, and don't you dare think of taking your brother's car. I told her I'll have supper later, took the car keys from this old floral ceramic Italian tea pot, and was off with the smoothest riding car to me in the world.

I arrived at the corner, and the five of us headed to Howard Beach and the Bow Wow. When we got to the Bow Wow, I parked in their rear parking lot, and we all got out. You would think we hadn't eaten in a month. Big Davy was the first one to the entrance doors on the 163 Avenue side of the building, two three-foot wide large glass doors. The rest of us were right behind Davy when just before he opened one of the glass doors, he turned and told us all to hold it. We stopped dead in our tracks. I like knowing what the day will bring, what to expect, and when to expect it, and I knew this wasn't going to be good. Big Davy backed us off and told us that there were three motherfuckers inside that he hated. That alone was good enough for me. Apparently, when Big Davy was a kid and just moved into Cypress Hills Projects, these guys lived in the building next to Big Davy's building. They were older guys that had lived there and hung with the bros and fucked with all the younger white kids that lived in the projects. I told Davy and the guys to lean against the side of the building where they can't see them, especially Davy who they might recognize. Cars were also parked on the side of the Bow Wow fronts facing in about six feet from the entry doors. Sonny and I kind of leaned and sat on the hood of one of those cars. Sonny was on my right side. We waited for these three dudes to finish paying the bill and come outside. It took a while. One dick got up and went to the bathroom. We were all starving, and I worked my ass off today and had no lunch, and now I'm anxious, nervous, and pissed off. By this time in my life, I'm pretty much a destroyer, strong with accrued punching power. The guy came out of the bathroom, and the other two got up and went to the counter and paid their bill. They were talking and laughing, not suspecting a thing. The two large glass doors opened together, and now these three were about a foot and a half away, face to face with me and Sonny. I jumped off the car and discard the first dude with a vicious right hand that dropped him right where he stood, half on the sidewalk and half inside the Bow Wow. One of the other dudes ran right into Sonny. Sonny took him down and fucked up whatever complexion he may have had with a few kicks to the face. I liked Sonny's passion in war, and where I had intensity, Sonny seemed to be indifferent. The third dude ran to his right. Big Davy caught him with a quick hard right hand to the side of his head, knocking him into the entrance of the rear parking lot. We looked at one another and without saying a work knew we had to get the fuck out of there. We ran to the car. I turned the car on and put it into reverse, speeding back when everyone was yelling at me to stop. I stopped and said, "What the fuck is the matter?" They said you just missed running over the guy Davy knocked out. I put the car in drive and drove out the far entrance onto Cross Bay Boulevard, made a right turn and then the first U-turn I could make, and headed back to the Triangle. On the way back, I asked Big Davy, "What the fuck did you hit that dude with?" We had a good laugh. I had to have my hot dogs, so we went to Snider's deli, and I had my two franks on club bread with sauerkraut and deli mustard, French fries, and a Dr. Brown's Cel-Ray Soda. That was our original quest of the night. It's a shame that they probably never understood why they took such a seemingly senseless attack. It was like justified injustice (my core of existence).

New Lots Boys versus Pink Housing Projects

It was the summer of 1963. It was a Sunday morning. I had worked my ass off that week, installing carpet at the Holiday Inn on Sunrise Highway in Rockville Center, on Long Island, New York. I had been out pretty late the night before, Saturday. I had gone to the Village Vanguard, a jazz club on Seventh Avenue in Manhattan. None of my friends were in to jazz, so most of the time I would go by myself. Thelonious Monk, one of the best jazz piano players of that time, was playing, so I had to go. One thing about jazz and blues clubs was you could go alone, have a great time, meet some great people, and never have a problem. If you took away the political intrusions and added a little cool sound, people just got along whether they were black, white, or Hispanic.

Monk was so wasted that night that he fell off his piano stool three times before he was carried back to the bar. He was finished. The bartender put a drink in front of him. He looked at it, laid his head on the bar, and went to sleep. At least I heard him play a few bars. The Vanguard always had good talent hanging out, and that night was no exception. To my pleasant surprise, a guy stepped out from the bar, opened up the case he was carrying, pulled out an alto saxophone, walked over, and said something to the bass player and drummer. The bass player stepped up to the mic and to my surprise announced the gentleman as Sonny Stitt. I played the sax, but I was no Sonny Stitt. They put on a great show. The first song Sonny played was "Skylark," and it only went up from there. I was glad I went. I left the club at about 2:00 a.m. I was wide awake and thought I'd get a little something to eat, so I took a walk through Greenwich Village. When I got to the corner of Bleeker and Thomson Streets, there were so many people hanging out you would have thought it was the middle of the day. There was a little place off the corner where I could smell sausage and peppers. I headed straight for the aroma. I had to maneuver my way through a crowd of hippies; the times they were changing. Next thing I knew, someone grabbed me around my neck, and I knew from the touch it was a chick. At the same time she grabbed me, she put a big old hickie on my neck. I turned and saw, dressed in what I would call a potato sack, the cutest girl I had ever seen, with this big smile and bright hazel eyes. Her hair was long, naturally wavy, and brown with light golden tones, and she had a face full of freckles. I didn't have to put a name to this face; I knew her. I had dated her for a short time a couple of years ago. As beautiful as I thought she was, her behavior was destructive. When I had turned to look at her, she got right up close to my face. I could almost taste the fresh clean scent of peppermint on her breath. The first words out of her mouth were "Richie Q!" I looked at her and said, "Linda." The next words out of her mouth were "Sleep with me tonight." I felt a quick flicker of a smile crossed my face and just as quickly disappeared. She noticed it, looked at me, and said, "Do you feel threatened by me?" Right then and there, I had a flash back. Two years before, there was a bunch of us hanging out on New Lots Avenue one night. We were standing outside the Terminal Luncheonette. It was a beautiful Halloween autumn night. Twenty feet above us was the last stop on the IRT railroad. A train had just pulled up, and people were coming down, walking past us. Most of the people we knew from the neighborhood. For some reason, I looked up, and at the top of the stairs, I saw a girl dressed as Raggedy Ann, with braids, bright red hair, large freckles, a red and white plaid skirt, a button-down long-sleeved white blouse, with big patches on the skirt and the blouse, and a pair of red socks and brown shoes. She was holding this big old round rainbow lollipop. My friends started on her when she hit the bottom step. She looked at us and said, "Which one of you motherfuckers is going to walk me home?" One of my friends said, "Where do you live?" She said, "Fountain and Pitkin." To get to Fountain and Pitkin Avenue from New Lots Avenue, you had to walk through some of the worst areas in East New York. One of the guys said, "Are you nuts? Take a cab!" I said, "Come on, I'll walk you." Not really a great plan on my part, for me or any New Lots Boys alone, unless you had a death wish. We got to Fountain and Pitkin without incident. We dated for a few weeks, but by then, we were pretty intimate. I did like her a lot, but that was where it ended. I was a pretty straight-laced guy. My behavior was simple; I liked to work and have honest money in my pocket. I worked Monday, Tuesday, Wednesday, Thursday, Friday, and Saturday. I liked to hang out with the guys after my workout during the week. On Fridays, I liked to go to the clubs and look for chicks. Saturday nights were date nights, and I would usually have a date. Now Linda, on the other hand, was wild and liked her booze and drugs. I knew soon into our relationship that her life was headed for destruction, and there wasn't anything I could do. I had to end it with her. I told her how I felt. That night, she got drunk and wanted to fight with the toughest girl on New Lots. I told her she had to go home. She told me she loved me and was crying. I felt bad, but she was drunk or drugged up every night. Ralphie was a couple of years older than I was, and he had a car. I asked if he would mind taking her home. We drove her home, and I took her up to her apartment. Her sister Patty opened the door and put her to bed. Ralphie and I went back to New Lots. A week went by, and I didn't hear from Linda. It was a Saturday, and I was working at my uncle Frank's butcher shop. I looked up and standing in the doorway was Linda. She said, "Richie, can I talk to you?" I took off my butcher's apron and went just outside the front door. She looked beautiful in nice blue jeans and a black tank top with her hair down. I said, "I told you not to come back to New Lots again." She didn't say a word, just right handed me a shot in my nose, and then split, running down New Lots Avenue east toward Linwood Street. I ran after her and grabbed her by her hair, on the corner at the bus stop, and put her down. At that moment, the bus pulled up, and everyone on the bus was staring at me. I still had her by the hair. I looked up at the people on the bus and said, "Don't worry, I'm not going to hit her." I looked back down at Linda and said, "You have to stay off New Lots." She was crying. I felt like shit, but I had to send her home. She went home, and I went back to work.

So now I found myself face to face with her in the middle of Greenwich Village, thinking, "I can't go there." This gay guy walked up to us and told Linda that he had to take a piss. She told him to go take a piss in the ally across the street. It was now 3:00 a.m., and I told her to go watch that her friend didn't piss himself and that I had to be going. She gave me a big kiss on my lips and said she was there every night and asked me to please come back. I could see that she was wasted. I turned and left and went back to where I had parked my car. I went home thinking, "What a waste. We lived in two different worlds." I never saw or heard from her again. I'm sure she got caught up in the 1960s cultural degradation. I got home at about 4:00 a.m. There waiting up was my Italian mother, yelling at me that my older brother had been home since ten o'clock. The only thing that could stop her from yelling was "Ma, make me macaroni!" That did it! My mother could always make something to eat in minutes. I ate, washed up, and went to bed. The next thing I knew, she was waking me up for breakfast. I said, "Mom, it's eight o'clock on Sunday morning." She said, "So? Your brother's up!" So I had breakfast, took a shower, got dressed in a pair of jeans, a white T-shirt, and a pair of sneakers, figuring I'd get more sleep in Elton Street Park. Just before I left the house, the phone rang. My mother picked it up and said hello, then handed it to me saying, "It's one of your bum friends from New Lots." I took the phone. It was Arnie. He said, "Q, we've got to talk. It's important." I told him I'd meet him in the park. I walked to the park; it was about a fifteen-minute walk from my house. When I got there, Arnie was there with Foxy. I said, "What's up?" They said, "Big Davy and a few of the guys got jumped at St. Fortunata's Feast last night by this big white dude, Frankie, and his bros. They hang out at the Pink Housing Project. The two best feasts in East New York were St. Fortunata on Crescent Street and Linden Boulevard and St. Rita on Liberty Avenue.

Every summer, all of East New York would look forward to the feast. We always went for the sausage and pepper, zeppalas, games, and rides and to check out the ladies. This one night, Frankie G, an Italian dude that hung with the bros from the Pink Housing Project and his cronies and other bros from Cypress Hills Housing Projects were at the feast. The Triangle was about one mile from the church. Frankie and his crew were there when the New Lots Boys showed. I wasn't there, so I don't know exactly how it went down. What I do know is that the New Lots Boys were way outnumbered. Big Davy had a cast on because he had a broken hand, which left our guys with an even bigger disadvantage. Now, mind you, Big Davy was six feet two and two hundred and thirty pounds, a big guy that could bang with both hands and not someone you would want to fuck with. I wasn't new at this; I had already been through plenty of wars and was pretty established. If you fucked with one of our guys, then you fucked with all of us; we had our own street laws. Today, it's all about me; but in those days, growing up on New Lots, it was all about us! Even outnumbered, we had an advantage over other gangs in the area. New Lots Avenue had the East New York Boy's Club on Ashford Street, a few feet off New Lots Avenue, where we would mostly hang out in the winter months, play basketball, hit the heavy bag and the speed bag, and just kick the shit out of each other until we drew blood; in our book, this was fun.

Sally pulled up to Elton Street Park with his car. He said, "What's up?" Foxy said, "We have a problem we have to take care of with this guy, Frankie, at the pink houses." Sally said, "Let's do it! I'll drive." On the way, I told Sally to drop us off at the Pink Housing Project park and wait with the car in the street. If Frankie was there, he'd definitely be with his bros. Foxy was half Italian and half German, Arnie was Jewish, and I'm Italian. Foxy and Arnie were naturally tough guys, with lots of heart, and I worked at being a bad dude. We got out of Sally's car and walked into the pink housing park. Arnie was carrying a three-foot pipe, Foxy had a pipe about one foot long, and I worked hard at striking with accuracy, whether I threw lefts or rights; I hit my target. There were a couple of dozen bros in the park, some hanging out, others playing basketball, and one large white guy sitting at a chess table with about six of his bros. One thing I knew for sure was that Foxy and Arnie would fight to the death; I didn't have to watch my back or give it a second thought. I didn't know Frankie, but I had a pretty good description, and he was the only white guy in the park. Foxy had also told me that he spoke like a Bro. We walked straight to where he was sitting. Arnie was on my left and Foxy was on my right. When we got up to where he was sitting, he looked up at us with this cocky attitude. He looked right at me and said, "What the fuck ya looking at, my man?" I asked him if he was Frankie G, and he said it again, "Who's asking, my man?" I'm not sure he got that whole sentence out before I put my left foot on the bench he was sitting on. I lifted myself up onto the bench with my left foot and kicked him in the head with my right foot. As he was going down, I threw him about four straight right hands, knocking him out and to the ground. His cronies jumped back. I picked him up off the pavement, put him up against the park fence, and told Arnie to crack this motherfucker's head. It wasn't very pretty, but by this time, I had seen the other side do some really ugly stuff. Foxy was just standing there. By this time, everyone stopped playing ball, and they were just staring at us. Foxy just looked up and said, "So you're gonna stand there and let your man take a fucking beating? Nice! Well if he lives, tell him New Lots; and if he grows any kind of balls, my name is Lord Fox." We walked out the same way we walked in. Sally drove us back to the Triangle. I had to go home for Sunday dinner with my family. I called Big Davy and told him what had just gone down. He lived in Cypress Hills Housing Project, so I also told him to watch his back. I heard Frankie went to the hospital. He lived, and we never heard from him or his bros again. So now I was home in my kitchen listening for a half an hour to my five-foot, ninety-pound Italian mother, hitting me with her wooden spoon and yelling that everyone was waiting for me to eat. My brother was already eating. My father was on his chair in the living room out cold. I sat down to eat ziti with meat sauce, pig's feet, neck bones, and braciole, sausage and meat balls. At present, my mother is ninety-five years old and can still kick this tough guy's ass. And the world did change. Three months later, on November 22, 1963, JFK was assassinated.

New Lots Boys versus the Events of June 1964

In the summer of 1964, on a perfect Sunday morning, Mom made breakfast. I took a shower, got dressed in my fight gear (white T-shirt, blue jeans, and tan desert boots), and was bored to death. The night before, my friends and I went to the Community Gardens in Springfield Gardens, Queens, New York, a large dance club with lots of young ladies.

The guest entertainment for the night were the Ronettes, three lovely young ladies with great vocals and one of the more popular girl groups at that time. That night, the girls were great; the stage they were on was about four feet off the dance floor. One of the girls had gotten a little too close to the edge of the stage. That's when Foxy reached up, pick her up off the stage, planted a big kiss on her lips, and then placed her back on the stage.

The girls were nice about it and didn't seem to mind; they even laughed about it. All the bouncers ran up to the stage and went to grab Foxy, telling him he would have to leave the club. We all ran up to where Foxy was. Foxy told these guys we were leaving anyway, and he told the lead bouncer that if he touches him again, he'll knock his fat ass out and he and my friends will tear the place apart. We walked out without incident. The next week, my friends went back and banged out a few bouncers, and the rest were gone.

So on this beautiful Sunday morning, I headed out to New Lots Avenue to see what my friends were doing. I got there early in the morning, and there was Arnie sleeping on the park bench at the small triangle like he was sleeping in his bedroom. Arnie didn't have much of a home life and was mostly living on the streets. I woke Arnie up and made him wash up at the terminal luncheonette on Lavonia Avenue under the IRT train trestle. I bought him breakfast. Then I heard "Hey, Q, what's up?" There standing in the doorway of the terminal was Frankie B. At age seventeen years, he was pretty gone; hanging with him on the street was a gamble, not knowing what dark pleasures were on his mind.

After breakfast, Arnie said he had to meet Johnny Reb at the pizza place on Van Sicklen Avenue across PS 166 George Gershwin Junior High School at noon. I told Arnie to come and take a walk, and as we were walking out of the terminal, Frankie B accompanied us. The pizza place where we were meeting Johnny Reb was about a mile away. With these two guys, it didn't take much perception to know that this is going to be a prescription for disaster. If I needed any two guys to go to war by my side, it's these two.

We walked west on New Lots Avenue to Van Sicklen Avenue, made a left, and walked just past Hegeman Avenue when Arnie grabbed me by the arm. I said, "What's up?" He was staring halfway down the block on the west side of Van Sicklen Avenue across the street from where we were. Arnie said, "There is that motherfucker Zorro." Zorro was the leader of the El Tones, and Arnie and Zorro went to PS 166 at the same time, before Arnie was a New Lots Boy. Arnie told me that Zorro and around ten El Tones jumped him outside of school and fucked him up really bad. Arnie looked at me and said it's payback time. I looked at Arnie and said, "So this piece of shit is yours now."

Zorro was walking north on Van Sicklen Avenue with this cute young Latin lady. When Zorro saw the three of us crossing the street, he knew he was in trouble. Just before he got to the corner of Hegeman Avenue, he turned and walked into a three-story brick apartment building. In front of the building, there were a few park benches on two sides against three-foot wrought iron fences leading to the entryway to the apartment building. Sitting outside were a few older men and women talking, enjoying the nice sunny day. Zorro walked through the front entrance doors, but he would have to be buzzed in to get through the lobby door. Arnie couldn't get to Zorro fast enough. The three of us ran into the foyer of the building, and without a word, Arnie ran up to Zorro throwing punches. Zorro hit the ceramic tile wall. Zorro's girl was screaming and cursing us. I yelled to her to get the fuck out of here. As she was running out, Frankie B grabbed her by her hair and dragged her out the door. Zorro was down, and Arnie was still banging him when I heard screaming outside. When I looked, I saw Frankie had Zorro's girl at the curb under a parked car, and he was kicking and bending over her, banging her with right hooks. The older people outside were yelling and calling us animals. I'm sure it looked disgusting, and Frankie B made it an absolute disgrace. I ran outside and grabbed Frankie B and said, "What the fuck are you doing?" He wouldn't stop, and I had to rip him off her. Arnie ran out, and we split back to the Triangle.

Frankie laughed all the way back, and Arnie and I were like "What the fuck is wrong with you?" We both knew he lost his soul years ago. I had to go home. I never look too far into the future, and what Frankie B did made me feel the future was lost. This was no victory.

When I got home, my mother told me Big Davy called. I called him back and told him what happened with Arnie and Frankie B. He said, "How many times do you have to learn that lesson?" I shook my head. Davy told me that a friend of ours, Freddie, was playing pool on Flatbush Avenue for big money. Big Louie was going to be there with a few of our friends. I wasn't a pool player, but I needed to get out. I took a shower; had dinner; and put on a new pair of charcoal slacks, a short-sleeved Italian black knit shirt, and a pair of black suede buck loafers. I met Davy on New Lots Avenue, and then we took the bus to Flatbush and got a transfer to the Church Avenue bus. We were walking west on Church Avenue, and walking east on our side of the street were two Puerto Rican guys. As they got to us, one guy yelled, "Hell Burners, motherfucker!" They were another Puerto Rican Brooklyn street gang. Big Davy had a cigarette in his mouth. He took it out with his left hand and said to the one guy with the big mouth "Hell Burners" as he stretched out his right hand to shake this dude's hand. This dude put out his hand. Davy grabbed his hand, pulling him inward, flipping his lit cigarette in the dude's face followed by a quick straight left and a devastating straight right hand, putting him to sleep.

The friend he was with began running west toward Kings Highway, a six-lane road with heavy traffic both ways. I was in hot pursuit as he ran across the highway, bobbing and weaving cars. I caught up to him and grabbed him by his shirt. He made a quick stop and went down. I was right on him now in motion, tripped over him, landed on my knees, and slid. This prick got up and ran. Cars were coming at me from every direction it seemed. I jumped up and ran back to where Davy was. He asked me if I was OK. I told him, "Fuck this day. Let's go the fuck home." My brand-new pair of slacks was torn on both knees, and when I got home and took my pants off, I saw how fucked up my knees were, and I had to go to work the next day laying carpet. I have to believe something other than myself controlled the events of this day. My work week was ugly. I put gauze and pads on my knees, and it still didn't help.

By the next weekend, I was just about feeling better, and my knees were healing but still a little tender. It was a Saturday. I was off from work and happy about that. It was a nice warm day, so I went to the Triangle to see what the guys were up to. By this time, I got to know the guys from Hemlock and Sutter and the Crescents, and we became pretty good friends. When I got to the Triangle, the only guys from my crew were Arnie and Sal (we called him Sailor). Arnie asked if I had plans for the day. He knew that I was always working and I would not let a good day go to waste.

One of my pet perks was to walk through East New York, visiting the other white gangs and their ladies. I told Arnie and Sailor that I was going to take a walk to Hemlock and Sutter, so the three of us walked up to Sutter Avenue then east. When we got to Crescent Street, one block before Hemlock, there were a few of the Hemlock and Sutter guys, Billy, Angel, and Tommy Simple. We were talking when three duds walked up to us and asked Billy, "Where the fuck are these guys from?" Billy said New Lots. The one guy doing all the talking looked us up and down before saying, "I thought the New Lots Boys were tough guys. These three look like fags." We were standing in the street next to the curb; Arnie hit this guy with a right hand, putting him down on the sidewalk, and one of the other guys grabbed me moving forward. I tripped on the curb and hit the sidewalk. A few more guys came, and Billy and his crew broke up the fight and said to us, "There is a vacant lot south on Crescent Street at the end of the block. Why don't you finish it there?"

The guy I was fighting had a big mouth and yelled out that he wanted this motherfucker, pointing at me. I was thinking just maybe he has something. I was also thinking I'm going to damage this piece of shit. This dude pushed my buttons, so I will not show any compassion, I will not hate, I will accept this challenge, and I desire this challenge. I will apply what I have learned. It would be thrilling, and I will be a savage without hate. As we walked, I sucked air into my lungs, and I did not say a word. When we walked down into to the vacant lot, this guy put up his hands in a boxing stance and said a few choice words just before I knocked him out with a vicious straight right hand that went clean through his flimsy awkward pose. Sailor was having a hard time with the guy he was fighting, so I ran up to this guy and cracked him in the back of his head; at the exact same time, Sailor cracked him with a straight right hand and it was good night. The guy Arnie was fighting was down, and Arnie was kicking him in the head while he was in a fetal position. My guy was still asleep; Billy looked at me and said, "I have never seen anyone get hit like that before." I said, "Billy, do you think that this scumbag deserved it?"

So I rejoiced in this noble act, and we all headed back to New Lots. When we got back to the Triangle, Hi Ho was there. I told him what happened. He was pissed; he loved to be where the action was. Hi Ho told me that he had to go to Long Beach tonight to his friend Freddie M's house.

So I went home, washed up, and my mother had dinner. I ate light, got dressed in my fight gear, and went out to meet our guys at the Triangle. When I got there, Hi Ho, Louie, Freddie M, Big Davy, Charlie Tarzan, Sandy Mick, Anthony S, and Schmidt and his Schmidt mobile were there. We jumped in the Schmidt mobile and headed to Long Beach. When we got to Long Beach but before we went to Freddie's house, we stopped in a pizza place and had a couple of slices of pizza each.

We were feeling good as we walked out of the pizza place and headed back to the Schmidt mobile. There were four huge bodybuilders walking behind us. Long Beach is a pretty nonviolent area, so we were comfortable and not expecting trouble. Louie P and Big Davy were bringing up the rear. Louie turned and noticed one of these guys was walking funny behind Davy, making fun of the way Davy was walking. Louie turned to Davy and told him what was going on. Davy turned and saw this dude laughing at him. Now we were all aware of what was happening. Big Davy cracked the guy with a straight right. I know Davy hits hard, but this guy hardly moved and lunged forward to grab Davy. I ran in throwing four straight right hands then grabbed him by this woven knit sweater he was wearing and spun him around with my left hand, ripping the sweater over his head while still throwing right hands. He was blinded by the sweater being pulled over his head and was backing up into a small open alcove of a bank. As he struggled to gain his footing and mount a defense, he stood straight up. I still had the sweater over his head. I hit him with two straight punches. I let go of the sweater and caught him with a quick left hook, and as he spun to his left, I threw a straight right flat-footed kick to his midsection. He flew off his feet and went straight through the glass entry door of the bank; at the same time, Anthony S went to hit him in this small space with a metal garbage can, cracking me in the head. I turned to Anthony and said, "Are you stupid?"

Years before, all of us younger guys and girls from New Lots would go to St. Gabriel Church dances on Friday nights. It became kind of a private event for the New Lots young teens. This one night, the entertainment was an Elvis impersonator, the first I have ever seen. My friends brutalized this poor guy. Then six Puerto Ricans walked in. Suddenly, there was complete silence. The only sound was the music playing. This was not good. The Puerto Ricans sat in one corner of the room, pointing and laughing. I don't know what they were thinking. We outnumbered them three to one. When one PR got up and asked one of our girls to dance, again what the fuck are they thinking? It was on. I stood back as my friends punished these guys.

One PR ran, trying to get out. I was standing near the entrance. He was headed right at me. I moved forward, and he ran into a straight right hand; at that same time as he was going down, Anthony was chasing him with a metal folding chair. He swung the chair to crack this dude and caught me on the top of my head. I had this immediate huge bump on my forehead with misty eyes and a weakness in my legs as I looked at Anthony and said, "Are you stupid?" So now, Anthony had cracked me in my head twice.

I got a little offtrack. Anyway, as I was saying, the dude went through the bank window, and the alarm went off. I found I had this dude's sweater in my right hand. I turned to split, jumping over two bodies laid out by my friends. We ran back to the Schmidt mobile and headed to Rockaways' Playland a few miles away then back to New Lots. I put on the sweater that I took, it just about touched my ankles. When we got back to New Lots Avenue, Robbie the Rogue was at the Triangle. I gave him the sweater. He was the only guy that I thought it might fit, but it was long on him.

I had gone to bed that night feeling pretty good. I got up early; it was Sunday. I had breakfast, showered, got dressed, and headed to the Triangle. The only one of my friends on the corner was Frankie B. He told me he was up all night getting wasted with Bobby Chick, Mouse, and the Mick. He said that he had to go to his grandmother's house on Blake Avenue and pick up a package for his dad. He asked me to take a walk, so we headed up Ashford Street on this beautiful Sunday morning. I was feeling good, and apparently not one of my senses kicked in, sixth sense or common sense, walking anywhere with this by now hopeless individual. As we approached Dumont Avenue, two PRs ran up to us. I knew one of them as the karate kid warlord for the El Tones. He had a revolver in his hand and ran up to Frankie and stuck the gun in his face yelling, "You maricon (fag in Spanish) motherfucker!" I was standing on Frankie's left; there are those times when one doesn't think and just reacts. I hit the dude with a smooth clean left hook. He didn't see it coming and took the full impact. It felt to me like I broke his neck. He went down and was reduced to an embryo. His friend turned and split, so did Frankie and I. We ran back to the Triangle. I asked Frankie what was that about. He told me that last night, that Mouse put a gun to this dude's head and pulled the trigger, and the gun misfired. The guy split yelling, "I'll be back!" I said, "So you left that shit out before you asked me to take a walk." (When will I learn?) I guess in spite of the dangers, I had to do what I had to do.

A good friend of mine Devo, came in from Kansas State University, he had gotten a football scholarship, while attending John J High School in New York.

There were guys in our neighborhood that weren't New Lots boy. They were the neighborhood athletes and they challenged us to a football game. I had no clue how to play football. For one week Devo trained the New Lots crew how to play.

Every day we met in the Linwood street side of the park. Devo and Mr. McGrane (the Micks father) trained us till they thought we were ready to meet the challenge.

We met on a Sunday at a ball field on the Conduit and Cross bay Boulevard. Devo, Mr. McGrane and two coaches from the other team, coached the game.

They were a top high school team in the area. The challenge was for an organized full contact game, with pads, helmets and body gear.

Devo said we had learned fast. He put me in a running back position. Sal. V was the quarter back.

On the first play the ball was past to Sal, he ran a few feet before he was tackled. He went down, got up yelling that his arm was broke. One of the coaches had to take Sal to the hospital..

'I'm thinking. This game is much too violent, and I have to go to work the next day.'

The next play I was handed the ball, I ran the field bobbing and weaving before I was stopped, about ten feet from the end zone. The coaches' blow there whistles and the play was died. I didn't go down, I was standing waiting for these guys to get off me. Devo ran over yelling. "The play is dead, let him go."

They all let go except this one guy trying to pull me down, by getting me in a head lock. He was determined to get me on the ground. Finally I had enough of him trying to break my neck, I spun around, grabbed him by his face mask, pulled his head down, throw and uppercut and two straight right hands.

Devo said. "They were the loudest punches he has ever heard. He was lucky he had a helmet on." I held him by his face mask. He went limp, so I slowly set him down on the ground.

Their team quiet, so in order to continue the game I had to go over and apologies. I did. Devo tried to explain to me, that it's okay to tackle, and not at all necessary to punch out the apposing team.

We did continue the game. We won eighteen to six. Our prize was the football. We hand delivered it to Sal.V at Linden General Hospital.

I think after the knock out. The heart was takin out of the apposing team. There defeat was our hollow victory. (Mr. Nero once told me that if you learn from your defeats you are a winner).

That night, a few of us guys (Big Louie, Hi Ho, Big Dave, Foxy, Arnie, and I) went to the corner and planned to go to Greenwich Village while Devo was still in town. What I remember was that before we went to the village, we took the subway to the Union SQ train stop. We walked up into the street, and there we saw a crowd of people standing and listening to someone speaking at Union SQ Park. As we got closer, we could hear the speaker denounce America and our democracy. That was the first time I ever heard that kind of talk about America. My friends were pissed and disrupted the speaker a little while, and then we headed to Greenwich Village.

No sooner had we got into the Village than there were about ten bros walking past us in the opposite direction. As they just got past us, one dick said something to me. I had one of my hands in my pocket, and this dude said, "I reckon you've got a gun in yo pocket, cracker?" That was the first time I heard the word cracker. I said to myself, "What the fuck is a cracker?" I said excuse me as I walked closer to him. He said, "Answer me the question or I'll kick your worthless hide!" As I threw him a kick to his groin and when he bent over, I cracked him on the back of his neck with a beautiful straight right hand, smashing him into the sidewalk. I looked up and saw Louie through this white girl halfway across the street. The girl had jumped on his back trying to scratch him. Devo had taken a car antenna off one dude and was whipping the shit out of him. They all split; the guy I knocked out was still asleep. We decided to go back to the corner. That was our village walk.

The next day, I went to work and was feeling good. My knees were finally healed, but now my hands were sore after these last couple of weeks, so I decided to take it easy this week and not work out. It was Monday. I got home from work early, took a shower, and had a light dinner. I wanted to go to the corner and relax and hang out. I had eaten light and dressed in my fight gear. This attitude I now have was my normal development after my many street wars.

When I got to the Triangle, there were dozens of guys hanging out, the older guys, the younger guys, and a few of my crew. Charlie Tarzan was there. I asked him where our guys were. He said all our crew went to the Sea View Bowling Alley. There were Puerto Ricans fucking with the kids that hung out in the bowling alley, and they thought they would catch a few PRs there. He said they left the corner about half an hour before he got there, and he had been there about fifteen minutes.

It was a nice night and a good one-hour walk to the bowling alley, which was on Flatlands Avenue on the border of East New York and Canaries. When we got there and walked inside, there was Arnie and a few of our guys. It didn't take but ten minutes after we got there when this crew of about ten PRs and their girls burst in, being loud and posturing. There was about ten of our crew plus a few Canaries guys there.

We made their whole crew get inside the bowling alley before a few of our guys closed off their retreat, the rest of our guys and the Canaries guys had the PRs boxed in. We were battle tested, and by this time, we had learned and were improved, mostly by staying tight and hanging together.

I zoned in on the guy at the head of this pack, and it was on. They were caught totally by surprise and were trying desperately to retreat. A few did get outside. Arnie, Tarzan, and I gave chase. When we got outside, the cops were already in the parking lot in front of the bowling alley. Everyone was now running out in every direction. Arnie, Tarzan, and I ran straight across Flatlands Avenue where it was dark and deserted and was in a few square blocks of car junkyards. When we got to the next corner, we slowed down. I turned to look to my right and saw three PRs walking on the opposite corner. I yelled mirar (look in Spanish)! They looked and started to walk in our direction. It was dark, and by the time they saw us three white boys, they turned to run. We took off after them. Arnie was lightning fast and caught up to the last guy; we dragged him into one of the junkyards and threw him on this huge mountain of car batteries. This dude kept yelling that he would be back with his boys and fuck us all up. Arnie worked him over a little. I told Tarzan to damage this piece of shit. Tarzan loaded up with a straight right hand, missed, and hit the batteries. My hands were hurting as it was, and now, after knocking out a couple of dudes in the bowling alley, just the sight of Tarzan hitting those batteries made my hands ache. I told Tarzan that this guy said he's coming back to fuck us up. Tarzan unloaded with lefts and rights. We left this dude in a pile of batteries drenched with blood.

I find myself always willing to pay the price for victory. Till the end, I will keep up my warrior training so my sword will always be at my side.

NEW LOTS BOYS VERSUS FULTON AND ROCKAWAY

It was 1963. There was an Italian street gang from Fulton and Rockaway. Unlike most of the unorganized street gangs in East New York, this gang was organized, working for a made guy, Fat Andy, an old school soldier with the Gambino organized crime family. I read an article by Jerry Capeci that said Fat Andy hated rats who became informers. Fat Andy's son, Anthony Jr., followed his old man into the life. His son testified and was a witness at the murder and racketeering trial of the mobsters who took over his father's crew. The Hollywood myth is that these people were men of honor, and people all over the world believe this bullshit. It's just Hollywood propaganda! You start in the business by being a rat, extorting hardworking family businesses, stealing, killing as only a coward can kill, from the shadows, dealing with drugs, and absent of any virtue or morality. But then to have your son come into the business of rats, blood, and guns, leading to a hopeless road and shame, can your moral account be any more overdrawn? Fat Andy died of a heart attack less than two years after his release from prison. I was eighteen years old by then. The only thing I knew about those guys was that years before I was a New Lots Boys, they had trouble with our older guys. John Gotti and the Fulton Street crew had this big rumble with Tony Cuccia and the New Lots Boys. I heard that they had met at the Old Mill, which was a part of East New York, at the very southeast end of Brooklyn. All I knew was that they fought. New Lots was kicking ass when John Gotti pulled out a shotgun and fired it in the air. The cops came, and everyone took off. Another time, Fulton and Rockaway came down to the Triangle with cars full of guys and got into this huge rumble with the New Lots Boys again.

The New Lots crew did some real damage. One of the Fulton Street guys came down in his brand new 1958 Chevrolet Impala; Tony Cuccia jumped in his car, drove it down Livonia Avenue, and drove it into one of the steel columns that held up the train trestle. Another one of the Fulton Street guys had to go to Riverdale Hospital that night. The hospital was on New Lots Avenue. That night, the New Lots Boys went to the hospital and gave this guy another beating right in the hospital. By 1963, the Fulton and Rockaway crew were pretty established in organized crime, loan sharking, gambling, extortion, stick ups, and highjacking at Idlewild Airport, later renamed John F. Kennedy International Airport. Most of the older guys from New Lots had moved on. My friends and I were now older and the best street fighters that the New Lots Boys ever had. Most of us guys trained to street fight in the East New York Boy's Club. The New Lots Boys were unorganized, and we were still street fighting bros and Puerto Ricans. Until today, East New York hasn't changed much, mostly a black and Spanish community. If you read the New York newspapers, like the *Daily News* or the *Post*, there are murders weekly from gang shootings, domestic violence, innocent children getting shot by stray bullets, and teenage mothers throwing their newborn babies into the garbage. I was fourteen years old when my uncle Frank told me to make a meat delivery to Crescent Street, about a mile from New Lots and the butcher shop. He had a couple of good customers there. I got on my larger than I was butcher bike, rode down Sutter Avenue, and had to pass Cypress Hills Housing Project to get to Crescent Street. Not a good idea for a little white boy with a basket full of choice meat. On the far left side of the project, there was a vacant lot. As I rode my bike east on Sutter Avenue, and just before I got to the vacant lot, I could see a bunch of people in the street, cop cars, and an ambulance. I stopped to look, and I saw Big Davy's father. I asked, "What's going on?" He said someone had thrown out a newborn baby. As we were looking, I saw a police officer take what looked like a toy doll out of a card board box; it didn't look real. The powers that be let East New York burn years ago and never tried to put out the fire.

Now I'm eighteen years old, and I had the world by the balls. I was still working out every day, going to work, and putting honest money in my pocket, and I thought that I had the best life. Looking back, I did! My war was still in front of me. At that time, all I knew about the older guys from Fulton Street was they had most of the unorganized white street gangs in East New York pretty bullshitted. Most of the older crew from New Lots and other white street gang members had moved on, gotten married, had jobs, and knew that they had to move out of East New York to bring up their children in a better community. East New York was on the far eastern end of Brooklyn, bordering Queens, the gateway to Long Island. Most of the white community from East New York exited to Long Island. You could buy a single family home, live on a safe block, and send your kids to a good school the American dream.

It was the fourth of July, a beautiful midsummer's day. I had called a young lady I had met at the Colonial House, a bar on city line, where most of the guys and girls from East New York would hang out. By this time, we all pretty much got along. She told me her name was Jo Jo. I talked to her for a while and finally got up the nerve to ask her for her phone number. She was a beautiful young lady, with light hair, big bright light eyes, and a big beautiful smile. I had to get to know her. I had called her to see if she wanted to come over to my house. She had this little Italian sports car. She came over, and we hung out in my basement. I put on some music, and we talked. I thought she was lovely, and we had some laughs. Everything was going great when my mother called down to say that I had a phone call. I excused myself and went upstairs. My mother handed me the phone. It was the Mick, Mike Mcgrane, a good friend. His mother was Italian and his father was Irish. I remember how they would walk together with their dog, holding hands. You didn't see moms and dads in those days showing that kind of public display of affection and warmth; I thought it was great. The Mick had five sweet beautiful sisters, and then there was the son, the Mick, a very troubled, complex young man with great artistic talent. When I picked up the phone, the Mick told me he needed my help with some guys at the house next door. They were shooting off fireworks and some were landing in his backyard. I told Jo Jo that I had to go and help the Mick with something. I didn't have a car at that time, so I asked Jo Jo if I could borrow her car. She gave me her keys, and I told her I'd be right back to hang out. I took off. The Mick lived on Atkins Avenue, across the Street from PS 202, between Hegeman Avenue and Linden Boulevard. When I got to the Mick's house, the Mick and his father were outside in front. There was a small vacant lot separating the Mick's house from the house next door. There were nine guys standing outside and a few women and children. I pulled up to the Mick's house, parked, and got out. The Mick was holding a pitchfork, and his dad had a bat. He handed me a machete. For a few minutes, no one said a word. I didn't know where they came from or recognize any of these guys. They looked like they were about in their midtwenties and thirties and Italian. They were talking to one another and giving us challenging stares. I walked forward, stopping halfway, and said, "There are nine of you and three of us. Do we have a problem here?" This guy picked up a young child in his arms and walked toward me, stopping about ten feet away. I put down the machete on the sidewalk and said, "Put the kid down." Without a word, he turned and walked back to where his friends were and handed the child to a woman. Two Cadillac cars pulled up, and four guys got out of each car. They were dressed nicely, and you could tell they were wise guys. Now there were seventeen dudes in a huddle. They were talking and looking at us. I picked up the machete and walked about ten feet from where they were standing. They were all staring at me and pointing. I said, "Hey, there are seventeen of you dudes. Do you think you have enough guys now?" I have to admit, I was somewhat uncomfortable. It was not the first time I had felt that way, but I had that machete in my hand. I was sure that they knew that was one fight they had to come to with guns, and they looked and fit the profile. This one guy looked at me and said, "You're going to need more than Tony Cuccia to get you out of this." Tony Cuccia, one of the older New Lots Boys, had a justified reputation of being mentally disturbed, from sticking up wise guy's card games, to shooting his good friend Stevie in the face, to his many crimes, which are too numerous to mention. He had lost his soul years ago. Later on, I found out that the guy I had been talking to was Nicky Carazzo. After John Gotti went to prison, Nicky became the acting boss of the Gambino family, along with his brother Joe Joe Carazzo and their very good friend Lenny Dimaria, a Gambino soldier. I said, "I don't need Tony Cuccia for this." Was I worried? Probably, but I don't remember. The odds weren't with us. I'd been there before. I didn't know where these guys came from, and I knew that it wasn't good. Nicky was at least four or five years my senior and had a young son, so why would he want to get involved in such bullshit with two young punks. But since Nicky was the spokesman, it seemed natural to zero in on him. I got this surge of pride; I liked it when the odds were against me, and at the price of my moral code, whatever happened, at least I could keep my soul. That crew was giving me nothing. I knew they couldn't be worried about two young punks and an old man. My anxiety was building, so I had to say something. They were still staring and talking when I said again, "Do you think there are enough of you dudes?" The eight guys that drove up got back in their cars and drove off. Nicky and his people went back in the house. I turned to the Mick and his dad and said, "I think they were afraid of us." And we had a good laugh.

In my heart, I knew we had just gotten a reprieve. To me it was over. I thought that they presumably thought "These two young punks aren't worth the headache." I told the Mick and his dad to call me if they needed me again, and I went back to my basement, and there she was, with that big cute smile on her beautiful face. It was all good! Little did I know of the tempest that lay ahead of me. After a couple of hours of hanging out with Jo Jo, she had to go home. We kissed good-bye, and I can still see that beautiful smile as she walked away. I asked her if she would like to stay for dinner, but she said her mom expected her home for dinner. I went upstairs where my mom was making dinner. My dad, brother, mom, and I were just about to sit down for dinner when the doorbell rang. My father got up to answer the door. When my dad walked back into the kitchen, he had this strange look on his face. Before I could say a word, he told me to go into the living room, which was just off the kitchen. He wanted to know what this guy wanted with me. I asked, "What guy?" He pointed out the window and said, "That guy!" Standing on my stoop was Tony Cuccia! My father was crudely abrupt, with this ugly physical effort which I had never seen in him before when he said to me, "What are you doing with that fucking nut job?" I said, "I'll take care of it." He went back into the kitchen. I went outside. I had never had any kind of relationship with this guy, other than hello or good-bye, and now he was knocking at my door. I knew this couldn't be good. When I got outside, he said hello. I said, "What do you want?" He told me that the guys I had trouble with that day wanted to talk to me. I said, "About what?" He said, "They just want to talk about the incident you had with them today. Meet me on New Lots Avenue tonight at around 8:00 p.m. I'll stay with you to make sure nothing happens." I asked him where those guys were from. He just turned, walked to a car waiting for him in the street, got into the passenger side, and said without turning "Eight o'clock!" When I went back inside and sat down to eat, my father said, "I know that guy. He's a screwball! Stay away from him!"

After I had eaten dinner, I called the Mick and told him that Tony Cuccia had come to my house and wanted me to meet him on New Lots that night to talk to those guys that you had a problem with today at your house. The Mick told me that a couple of guys had come over to his house, and one of them had put a gun on the table and told the Mick's father and him that they didn't want to hear from them or any of their friends again, or they would be coming back. To my surprise, the Mick told me that he had to look out for his family and that he couldn't get involved. Even at eighteen, I was still pretty naive. I said, "I understand. I'll take care of it," and hung up the phone. I thought about it, a gun on the table with my family there. Fear would be practical, and I believed I had fear; more than fear, I had anger. I had this unusual desire to move forward, and it seemed natural. At 8:00 p.m., I went to New Lots and met up with Tony Cuccia. When a couple of cars pulled up, my friends asked, "Where are you going with these guys?" Tony Cuccia said, "I'll go with him. It'll be all right." The guys in the car said, "No problem, we just want to talk." One of our older guys, Bush, said, "I'm going with Richie." I got in one car; Bush and Tony got in the other car. I really was that naive to think that these guys just wanted to talk. They drove to Atlantic Avenue, drove over the Atlantic Avenue overpass, made a U-turn on Eastern Parkway, and parked halfway down the block, alongside the Atlantic Avenue overpass. There were a few attached two-family houses with a few stone steps leading to the front door. It was dark and deserted.

When the car I was in pulled up to one of the houses, I saw the first car, with Bush and Tony Cuccia, was already there. Tony, Nicky, and a few guys were there, sitting on one of the stoops, waiting for us. I didn't see Bush. I found out later they had dropped him off along the way. Knowing Bush, he didn't go voluntarily. There were five guys sitting on the stoop with Tony Cuccia. There were four guys in the car I was in. We all got out. Now I was alone, standing in front of those guys. I had heard later, after my situation with this crew, that this was the way they liked the odds. There was me and Tony Cuccia and eight of them. By this time in my life, I could size up this crew. They were older, and just a couple of years ago, that alone might have made a difference. Not one of this crew threatened my instincts, so I focused on their lead guy, Nicky, who seemed to want to do all the talking. I looked at Nicky and said, "Do you want to talk to me?" At that moment, Tony Cuccia got up off the stoop and walked away, headed toward Eastern Parkway and their corner hang out, a luncheonette. As Tony turned his back and walked away, I said, "Go ahead, you fucking little rat." He never turned around. This was reality cutting across my mind at eighteen years of age. I had been there a dozen or more times before. They had the odds, so it wasn't a matter of if it was going to happen, but when. To me, this was dark pleasure. I worked harder than anyone I knew at street fighting. I knew I would get damaged, but this victory would be worthwhile. I turned to Nicky and said, with an exaggerated sincerity, "You're the talker, so how about you and me, dude?" In my pea brain, I was thinking man to man. I found out Nicky's motives when he said, "We don't deal that way." I said, "How the fuck do you deal?" At that, Nicky's friend Lenny pointed his finger in my chest. I smacked his hand down and stepped back out of the way and said, "I'll fight the two of you, motherfuckers." I heard from the side, "You tell the Mick that we'll burn his house down." I said, "Tell him yourself, hero." It was one of Nicky's younger brothers. Just then, I heard a couple of cars coming around the corner, off Atlantic Avenue. Five or six guys got out and ran up to where Nicky's crew and I were standing. It was Ralphie B, Big Davy, and a few of my friends. Fat Andy was yelling; he kept saying, "What the fuck are these punks doing here?" I heard Big Davy turn and tell Fat Andy to go and fuck himself. Apparently, the fat man had not a thing to say, just this permanent sneer on his face and a blinding hatred in his eyes, but not enough to say another word, another Gambino useless coward of a man who produced nothing.

Andy's crew couldn't backpedal fast enough. A single thought cut through my mind, with proud strength and a physical sensation of pleasure. They still had the odds, but without their firepower, they were defenseless. Nicky and his crew kept saying, "We're just talking. Everything's OK. We just had to clear the air and make sure there wasn't a future problem. We're all

Italians here, and we know you guys fight the niggers and the spics." I would have loved to see the result of that action. Nicky and his crew didn't seem to want any part of it. No one got hurt, just maybe a few egos. I believed Nicky when he said there wasn't going to be a problem. I don't think they needed street-fighting punks to interfere with their business. We shook hands and left. We went back to New Lots Avenue. To us, a handshake meant it was over.

Later that night, a few of us were walking on the avenue between Elton Street and Cleveland Street, on the south side of the avenue. It was a vacant area with a couple of billboard signs. We got caught by surprise when three carloads of guys pulled up and jumped out with bats and pipes. We were on the sidewalk. There were cars parked on the street in front of us. They jumped out and came at us from between the parked cars. We stood our ground. One guy ran up and yelled, "Who cursed Andy[Fat Andy]?" I guess they had to save face. My friend George H, at that time, was always drunk. He stepped forward and said, "Who wants to know?" This guy hit George in the face; I doubt he felt it. As soon as George got hit, Big Davy right handed that dude; he hit him so hard that the guy flew on top of the hood of one of the parked cars. It was on! When the action started and you were in the middle of it, you had no idea what was going on around you. I zeroed in. We were pretty outnumbered. Some guy with a bat came running at me. As he swung and tried to clip me, I faked and slipped to my left then caught him with a short left hook and put him on his ass. Another dude tried to pull the same thing. I grabbed him by his shirt, spun him around, and threw him down. As I had him down, banging him with right hands, something told me to look up. Running at me with a litter basket over his head was Nicky; he wanted my ass! When he saw me look up, and even before I could react, he threw the litter basket down and split; he knew I wanted his ass badly. I ran after him. I didn't get but a few feet when someone whacked me on the back. I thought it was one of Nicky's crew. This guy had run up on me. I turned and reacted with a quick right hand, and at the same time as my right hand caught this guy, I knew I was now fucked. As he went down, I saw it was a cop! I turned and saw another cop running for me. Now it was my turn to split. As I ran west on New Lots and toward Ashford Street, halfway down the block, there was Frank's Bar. Three other cops ran across the Triangle, blocking my way. As I turned to run the other way, the cop behind me came at me with his billy club. He raised the billy club to whack me, but I grabbed him, spun him around, and threw him into Frank's Bar. By now, there were cops all around me. Now I knew I was fucked big time! One cop grabbed me from behind by my neck, another cop tried to choke me, and there were so many cops they were in one another's way. Next thing I heard was Tony

Cuccia running up and yelling "Let the kid go!" The cops now turned to look at Tony. The one cop was still holding me by my neck from behind. I yelled at Tony, "You little motherfucker!" Next thing I knew, the cop holding me loosened his grip. I slipped from under his grip and split. I ran to the corner of Ashford and New Lots, made a quick left, and I was gone. Halfway down Ashford Street, I made a right and ran across the street, down a couple of alleyways, and came out on Barby Street. I ran south on Barby Street, crossed Linden Boulevard, and walked through the Boulevard Projects. When I got to Stanly Avenue, I sat on a park bench. My head was spinning. I knew I couldn't go home; if I did, it was sure jail time. I had to think. I didn't know what was going on with my friends. I wanted to go back to New Lots so badly but I knew if I did, I'd be fucked for sure. Race wars at that time, on New Lots Avenue, were weekly, and the Seventy-Fifth Precinct would send a dozen cops a night to patrol from Ashford Street to Elton Street along New Lots Avenue. The cops, instead of going to the precinct, went straight to New Lots Avenue in their own cars. Most of the cops parked their cars on Elton Street, between Hegeman Avenue and New Lots Avenue, alongside Elton Street Park, and walked to the Triangle. Nicky M, one of the older New Lots Boys, had just gotten out of jail. He was another one of those talented guys, a great artist, who lost his soul along the way to that criminal gene. When I was a young man, every time I ran into Nicky, we would talk. I liked the guy and his character.

I guess, for his sense of pleasure, he found out where the cops parked their cars and would sit in the park and watch the uniform cops get out of their cars. When they walked away, he would set their cars on fire. When the cops had had enough, they would go to the precinct, and a paddy wagon would take them to New Lots Avenue. Whatever Nicky's illusions were, we now had a dozen pissed off cops every night on New Lots Avenue. As I sat there, I knew this was serious; to me, it was the most serious feeling of my life, angry cops and wise guys. I was enjoying life, and now I was in a world of shit with these cannibals. I knew these people would not play fair. The voice within me told me that dealing with cops was a no win situation; dealing with Nicky's crew was a different story. I knew I couldn't go back to the avenue. I also knew I could not let myself be a target. A good percentage of the cops from the Seventy-Fifth Precinct and the wise guys were morally bankrupt. These were dark times. This was where we were as a society. I was cynical, and I knew in my mind, without a doubt, that these cowards would blindside me. I went to my cousin Tony's house. He lived on Elton Street, two doors away from me. He was home and invited me in. I told him the problem I had had that night on New Lots Avenue, with the Eastern Parkway crew and the cops. My cousin Tony was about fifteen years older than I was and was lightly connected. He was pretty familiar with Fat Andy's crew, and he told me to watch my back with those guys. There wasn't much justice for the hardworking honest man in East New York. Cynical logic told me, you fuck with me or my family, and I will burn you. (Death is certain for anyone born. Since this cycle is inevitable, I am not afraid. I find my strength in virtue and respect. My triumph will be to conquer or die. I believe in action and reaction, and I find revenge sweet.)

My cousin Tony had two 22 revolvers which he sold to me for $129.00 each. I had the money at my house. I asked him to go next door to my house and see if anyone had called. When he came back, he told me that the only one who called was my friend Foxy. I went next door, got my cousin the money, and called Foxy. He was home and told me what had happened and that I should stay away from New Lots Avenue for a while. One of the cops I hit had a broken jaw, and they were pissed and breaking everyone's balls. And as far as he knew, no one had given me up. I wanted to know about Nicky's crew. I needed some kind of heads-up on these guys. I told Foxy I had the two pistols and that there were three gas bombs under the train trestle on Hegeman Avenue. He said, "Good, we just may need them." I told him, "I don't want to get any of our friends involved. I knew where Joe Joe lived, on Sheppard Avenue, just off Hegeman Avenue, and if they or that little motherfucker Tony Cuccia go near or threatened any one in my family, I will first go after Joe Joe, then wait for that Fat fuck Andy and his crew to get comfortable in the Eastern Parkway luncheonette before I firebomb their punk asses." This was my awakening, not where I thought I would be at this time of my life. I was afraid but willing to except the end for my family or my friends, as long as I got my pound of flesh. Fighting the bros and the Puerto Ricans seemed natural, and my approach seemed clear, war. This seemed more devious. I despised my uncertainty. They were better at this than I was, and I knew this. I also knew the only means to compel men to action was fear. I had plenty of that and a sudden impulse to be vicious; I knew that was the only thing they would understand. That night, I stayed home. I thought, "Whatever is going to happen, I want to be here to deal with it." The next day, no one called or came to my house. In my heart, I wanted to go after these motherfuckers and deal the first blow. After a few days, I had gotten nothing from the cops or the wise guys. Foxy had called me and told me that Nino, one of our older guys from New Lots, talked to Nicky and his crew. He said that they didn't want a problem and they needed to know that I wasn't going to take this any further. I said, "That's OK with me." I never got touched. I did some damage, and that was OK. I still couldn't go back to New Lots Avenue for a while, at least until the cops moved on. I worked for Consumer Carpets and hung out at the PS 202 school yard. I never knew Nicky or Joe Joe that well. What I had heard about Nicky and Joe Joe, especially Joe Joe, was that they were smart and didn't need to associate or indulge with the likes of John Gotti. This guy just didn't get it. I did get to know Nicky and Joe Joe's younger twin brothers. I got drafted in 1965 and went to Vietnam. When I came back from Vietnam, after two years, East New York was infected. Organized crime had begun dealing more with the big money drugs. The honest, hardworking people that could afford to move out got out. East New York was in free fall. The guys I knew that were stand-up people were now dealing or dealing and doing drugs. The New Lots crew was now splintered. There were the dealers and drug addicts and the few that had kept their moral code, like Davy, Bruno, Jerry, Hi Ho, Ralphie, Sonny, Frenchie, Divo, and Louie, just to name a few. Then the few that had filtered into organized crime with the Gambino crime family, like Foxy, Arnie, and Johnny Reb, were the stand-up guys who I had liked and trusted. They had made the wrong choices and had paid with their life. Anthony Stabile, a low-life piece of shit who started out on New Lots Avenue, with his older brothers, fat Tommy and Rosario, went into the life of crime early, at sixteen. He came out of jail a bigger piece of shit then he was before he went in. When I came back from Vietnam, Foxy was hanging out with the crew from Eastern Parkway. As he put it, "I'm earning," and he was; Foxy had shown me $75,000 in cash; at that time, I was earning $160 per week. To me, there wasn't enough money in the world to make me respect or trust that life. I asked Foxy, "How can you trust these guys when you know their history?" Sonny told me a story that Foxy had been sitting in a car with a few of the guys from Eastern Parkway in a parking lot when a black uniformed watchman with a billy club told Foxy and his new crew to get the fuck off the property. Foxy said he thought to himself, "This dude is in big trouble." None of those guys said a thing. The watchman told them again to beat it and still nothing happened. Foxy then got out of the car, took the watchman's club, and gave him a beating with it.

It was the 1970s. I opened my first carpet store on Pitkin Avenue. Foxy would come by with his new crew and hang out for a while. They gave me carpet business, and they were nice guys to me. I carpeted Sally Ruggiano's whole house. Stephanie, his wife, was a very sweet young lady. Lola and I went to dinner with Sally and his wife one night, at Russo's Italian Restaurant on 101st Avenue in Ozone Park. To me, he was a smart and a nice guy, and I believe he could have been successful in any legal business he pursued. On May 6, 1982, Sally and Stephanie died in a suspicious plane crash on their way to Florida. I found out later that he was very heavily into the drug trade, making millions. He also introduced me to Gene Gotti, who I also found to be a pretty nice guy. He is now in jail doing big time, along with John Carneglia, again in the drug business. I knew John Carneglia originally from the wars we had with Hemlock and Sutter; he was a tough guy. He had a junkyard business on Fountain Avenue in East New York, and I had bought a few older cars there for my carpet business. In my opinion, here was another one of those guys who could have been successful in a legitimate business. I knew his wife, Helene, years before; she was a beautiful young lady. So why would you fuck this up John? You could have had a great life. Gene G and John Carneglia were also suspected of the actual hit on Big Paul Castillano and Biloitio. Unlike John's younger brother, Charles Carneglia, I heard later on, was a stone-cold killer for John Gotti. I didn't know Charles as well as his brother John. One day, while driving home from work down Fountain Avenue, just outside of John's junkyard, I saw Charles arguing with two bros. They were standing next to a young lady, trying to get into her parked car. She called to Charles for help and to watch her get into her car. As I was driving by and saw this, I made a quick U-turn, parked, and jumped out of my car. I ran up and asked Charles what was the problem. He told me, "These two motherfuckers were fucking with this girl." I told the girl to get into her car and told the bros to get the fuck out of there. They didn't say a word, they just left. Charles said, "Where did you come from?" I said, "That's East New York loyalty, cugino [Italian for cousin]." He thanked me, we shook hands, and I was gone. By 1965, the white gangs in East New York, with Hi Ho as a kind of ambassador, had the same agenda; our follies and loyalties still had to be experienced. Every white gang in East New York wanted and had an alliance with the New Lots Boys, and we would be there when called upon. Foxy asked me to take a ride with him. He had to go to this resort called Laurels, in upstate New York. Anthony C, Nicky C's kid brother, worked at the resort hotel, and these guys were giving him shit, so I took a ride. We met Anthony, and he pointed out the head guy, whom we took outside. Foxy said, "Motherfucker, do you have a problem with Anthony?" That dude's face was drained of color. He cried and begged Foxy to give him a break and said that it wouldn't happen again. Foxy told him, with a voice one tone lower than normal, and with his cold face and intense eyes, he said, "If we have to come back here again to deal with this bullshit, we will torture your punk ass." Anthony didn't have a problem after that. He got us a room in the hotel. Not an hour went by and I met a cute little Jewish girl named Sheila. She was sitting in the lobby of the hotel with a few of her girlfriends. The first thing I noticed was the large bangle bracelet on her right wrist. She looked unapproachable with her dark eyes. She was slender, with moist lips that gleamed in her young face. She was a very attractive young lady, and I had to meet her. I said hi. And she said, "Hi. Why don't you and your friend hang around?" We talked half the night. The next day, they were having a beauty pageant, and Sheila came in first place. I had a great weekend with a lovely young lady. On Sunday night, she gave me her telephone number. I kissed her good-bye. I had a 1965 Triumph TR4. Foxy and I got in my car and headed back home. I was back to being a fool again on my journey.

The second time I was wounded in Vietnam, I was sent to Japan to recuperate. Then I was sent back to Vietnam. I had kept in touch with Foxy. He had joined the Air Force and was sent to Saigon. On my way back from Japan, I flew into Tan Son Nhut Air Base in Saigon. I looked up Foxy. He was working at a clerical job in a huge airplane hangar. When I got there, I rang the buzzer on the door. It buzzed back, and I opened the door. I stood there in total shock! In a few days, I would be going back to my unit and back into combat. Now, in front of me, there I was looking at over a thousand new coffins and thinking, "One of these could be mine." I had to walk through the entire hangar to get the other side where Foxy had a desk; that was a great moment. It was the Christmas holidays, and since I had never had R&R, I decided to spend the holidays with Foxy. Every night for a week, we went into Saigon to visit and self-indulge with the young ladies. Then I had to get back to my unit. We said our good-byes, and I flew up to Pang Rang Base Camp for the 101st Airborne Division. In one day, they had me back with my unit in Kontum. Next thing, I got a letter from Foxy. He was in New York. He told me that when I had left him, he had gone to his commanding officer and told him that he wanted to join my unit and become a Recondo for the 101st Airborne Division. His commanding officer sent him to see a military psychiatrist. And the next thing he knew, he was discharged from any military duty. When I got home from Vietnam, I found a letter that Foxy had sent to my Mom and Dad after I had spent the week with him in Saigon.

"I never knew John Gotti, except what I've seen on TV or read in the newspaper, or heard from one of his associates. He thought he could run his new enterprise the old mafia ways; he looked to the old guard like Albert Anastasia. How did it work out for him? He took a bullet in the head. To me, John seemed to believe in all the Hollywood hype and he made all the same mistakes with his public arrogance, from his posturing, to his manner of dress. He just didn't get it. He was a degenerate gambler, having people eliminated, even people with families; so much stupidity, so many vices, so much error and sorrow. His biggest folly was having his son come into the business. A good friend of mine, Tommy Sneakers, was a body guard for John Jr. Years before, I would spar with Tommy and another good friend, Tony M., to keep sharp."

Tommy, to me, was a great guy and a tough young man. He's now in jail, like Foxy; he just didn't get it. Believe me, they were better than to get involved in that predictable business of grief. John Gotti's biggest mistake was making an outsider his underboss, a scumbag like Sammy "The Bull" Gravano. I don't blame him for turning on John. John's ego and loose tongue made Sammy believe he would be eliminated. I didn't know Sammy at all, but I knew his best friend Louie Malido. I met Louie through a mutual friend from a crew in Bensonhurst where I had a carpet store on Eighty-Sixth Street. I did carpet in his old house and then in his new house on Staten Island. I knew his family; his wife, Linda, was a very sweet, pretty young lady, and his children were the nicest kids. He had it all. Louie, from where I was viewing, seemed to be a nice guy and, unlike most of these guys, had a business sense and brains. At that time, I didn't know how involved he was. He did his own scumbag stuff.

As far back as the Mafia goes, that business has been a dead end; a hopeless road of vultures; they were greedy, self-indulgent, and predatory. It was theater; Hollywood wanted us to see this world as they would like us to see it, mysterious and enchanting, high living, and riches. John Gotti, like the Mafia leaders before him, had misused his soul. In the end, he lived his last days like a four-year-old child, being told when to go to sleep, when to get up, when to eat, when to go outside, or when to watch TV. In the end, he grew gray and suffered. Those people are the bottom feeders and the Italian humiliation. My greatest gift is my Italian heritage, together with its rich history and proud people, and in that lies my sanctuary. It seems to me that the Italian people in America will always be linked to the Mafia. It's up to you, the reader, to take back your heritage. You must thirst for knowledge and not from Hollywood's corrupted and conceited worthless orators.

All people should take pride in their explorers, scientists, inventers, artisans, and philosophers. In other words, discover the truth. (The truth in knowledge is salvation.)

New Lots Boys versus the Black Tops

It was late fall of 1963. I got a call from a good friend of mine, Stevie W. We were close in grade school at PS 202 seventh grade. At least one-thirds of the New Lots Boys were Jewish. Growing up in the New Lots area, half the population was Jewish, so we knew lots of Jewish kids from grade school that were not New Lots Boys or gang members. The New Lots Boys along with Johnny Reb and the Rebels for the most part kept the New Lots area, from Fountain Avenue to Pennsylvania Avenue to Sutter Avenue and to Wortman Avenue, safe from warlords and other street gangs from outside our area.

The young people in our area that weren't gang members for the most part did well in school and were generally nice kids. They would rent basements, mainly in the Flatbush area, to hang out at night and keep warm for the winter months. They were called frats. My friend Steve belonged to one frat just off Church Avenue in the town of Flatbush Brooklyn west from East New York and a little out of our area. He had called me and told me that these guys from Canarsie, Brooklyn, were coming down with their girls and fucking with me and my friends. He told me they are a street gang of mostly Italian guys called the Black Tops and they were from Canarsie, Brooklyn. He told me that they would show up on Friday nights. I always like Stevie, and I told him I'll be there with a few of my friends this Friday night.

So me and a few of my friends went to meet Stevie at this two story house; the house had a private door a few steps down into the basement. When we got there and walked inside, it was one large room and a little dark, with a couple of large sofas and chairs and a surprisingly beautiful light wooden floor. I'm in the flooring business. I never walk in a room without looking down at the floor. (Flooring people know what I'm talking about.) There were about ten of us New Lots guys and about twenty young boys and girls already there. They had music playing, and I remember the song that was playing when we walked in. (If you want to be happy for the rest of your life, never make a pretty woman your wife.) The kids there were pretty cool and were thanking us already, and nothing happened yet. They offered us soda and pretzels and potato chips. So we sat down and waited. I told Frank B that when these dudes come down and are inside, lock the door behind them so they can't get out. There were ten New Lots Boys; we definitely had this joyous sense of confidence and the element of surprise. I notice this cute young lady staring at me; when I looked up at her, she smiled and walked over and offered me a Coke or 7-Up. I took the Coke and thanked her. She said, "I want to thank you and your friends. I haven't been coming here because of these guys, and they treat our guys really bad." I knew they were embarrassed, and less and less kids were coming here. Last year, we had such a great time hanging out. I think her name was Shelly; she had a beautiful face, with long light brown hair with a plumpish figure. I just wanted to put my arms around her and hold her.

The very first time I felt that way was in PS 202. I think I was in the fifth or sixth grade when this young Puerto Rican girl from Cypress Hills Housing Project came into school; her name was Elsa T. She was soft-spoken, quiet, and the sweetest most exotic and beautiful young lady I have ever seen. I don't think I ever said one word to her. Let me just put it in simple language I was scared as shit to even look in her direction.

Now the door was closed but not locked. These scumbags just kicked open the door and walked in like they own the place, being cool in their black three quarter length leather jackets. There were around eight guys and a few maybe four or five girls. The guys walked in, and the dude in the lead was yelling, "We're here now, Jew boys!" Frankie locked the door behind them. You have to know that Frankie B, for a lack of a better description, was out of his fuckin' mind, scary at times. New Lots had more than its share of scary characters.

No sooner did this dude get the word Jew boys out of his mouth than Frankie cracked the dude in the back of the head with a short iron pipe. It was on, and Frankie was cracking even their girls. Within seconds, every one of these boys and girls were laid out. Now there are a few more Black Tops walking down into the basement. When they got to the door and saw what just happened, they turned and split. We went after them and caught up with these dudes at a Carvel ice cream stand parking lot just off Church Avenue. Charlie C was called Tarzan because he was huge, and this was before steroids. Charlie knocked this one dude clear across the hood of a car parked in the parking lot. It was over, and when we went back to the basement, the

Black Tops and their girls were gone. I thought the guy that Frankie hit with the pipe was done, unless they carried him out.

Shelly gave me a big kiss on my lips, and I got to put my arms around her. I was right. She felt so good I didn't want to let her go. Again, I was shy and still discovering the secrets of life, or in laymen's terms, "no balls."

After a few weeks, we heard a rumor going around that this guy Frankie C, one of the Black Tops, kicked my and Big Davy's ass. So about eight of us piled into Schmitty's Schmidt mobile, an old blue and white station wagon, and drove around Canarsie looking for Frank C and the Black Tops, not sure where they hung out. We knew they sometimes hooked up with another gang in Canarsie called the Avenue L boys, so we went to Avenue L. Not finding anyone, we drove up Rockaway Parkway to Glenwood Road, where there were guys hanging out at this corner luncheonette. The Sixty-Ninth Precinct was a block away, so whatever we had to do here had to be quick. We jumped out of the car, banged out a few guys, and got back in the Schmidt mobile. We didn't even know if these were the guys. To my friends, they were from Canarsie, and they were fresh meat.

Next, we drove to a bowling alley on Foster Avenue; there were a group of boys and girls hanging outside the bowling alley. Now Schmitty kept a rolling pin in the Schmidt mobile, and every time someone got whacked with the rolling pin, Schmitty would put a notch in it. Most of the notches in the rolling pin were made by Bobby Bear, the leader of Highland Park; once in a while, he hung with New Lots. He was another dude out of his mind. I don't know about brains; all I know is that he had balls, and we all seemed to like his character. So there were a few notches already on the rolling pin. We pulled up to the front of the bowling alley, and Big Davy asked if anyone knew a Frankie C. This guy walks over to the car and leans on the open window were Big Davy was and asked, "Who wants to know." Big Davy told the guy that he's a friend of Frankie C from school. This guy said that he went to school with Frankie. As he leaned closer, he said, "I'm Frankie's cousin, and I don't know who the fuck you are." Big Davy said, "Give him this message," and cracked this guy in the face with the rolling pin. We went back that night to the Triangle. Big Davy and I decided to go back the next day. The next night, I asked my dad if I could use his car, a 1951 off-white Ford with three on the column; it was a great ride. I picked up Big Davey at his house then drove to the Triangle to see if anyone wanted to take a ride. There was Hi Ho, Arnie, Stevie, Big Davy, me, and one of the guys from Hemlock and Sutter, Angel. They got in the car, and Hi Ho asked, "What's going on?" I said, "Davy and I have business to take care of in Canarsie." Without another word spoken, it was understood. I drove east on Flatlands Avenue not knowing were I'm headed. When we got to Remsen Avenue, I made a right turn heading north. When we got to Glenwood Road, I saw six dudes hanging out on a small three-step stoop in front of a grocery store. I passed them, made a U-turn at Farragut Road, and pulled up to where these guys were hanging out. Big Davy was on the passenger side. I was driving, and Hi Ho, Stevie, Arnie, and Angel were in the backseat. They don't have a clue of what's about to happen. Big Davy and I got out of the car and walked up to the front of the stoop.

Our guys still had no clue, but I knew if it goes down, they would be right there. I didn't know what Frankie looked like. There was one guy standing at the top step against a glass door, and his crew was hanging out alongside the grocery store steps. I walked up to the dude standing at the door and asked him if he knew a Frankie C. He said, "Yea, that's me. Who wants to know?" I put my left foot on the first step, pulled myself up, and hit this piece of shit with a straight right hand. He broke the window, and just before he went through the window, I grabbed him with my left hand and threw him onto the sidewalk. One guy was trying to jump over this green wooden fence. I tore him down and cracked him in the head and he was done. There was only one guy that had balls. He grabbed me by the collar of my jacket and threw me a right hand. I slipped and hooked him with a perfect left hook. Big Davy knocked out this dude in the street. Hi Ho and our guys were just about getting out of the car when I turned and told our guys to get back into my car, and we were gone.

Hi Ho was so pissed off at me for not letting him in on this, but I didn't know if these were even the right guys. You have to understand that most of our guys loved this, but Hi Ho lived for this, and for him to be left out was like sticking a knife in his heart. Hi Ho said, "I blinked, and there are three guys laid out on the sidewalk and one guy flies past me and lands facedown in the Street." We went back New Lots Avenue. We never saw or heard from the Black Tops again. My guilty secret is that it's in my blood. Each experience brings knowledge, so don't rush to judgment. (Let he who is without sin cast the first stone.)

New Lots Boys versus Canarsie Chaplains: Round 2

It was 1964. The day we met Arnie and he became a New Lots Boys, we met on Van Siclen Avenue, just south of Linden Boulevard, in front of Joe's Pizza, across the street from George Gershwin high school. It was a freezing cold night, and we were hanging out on New Lots Avenue, freezing our asses off as we did most winter nights. One of the guys said, "Why don't we take a run to Joe's and have a piece of hot pizza?" It sounded good to us. I had my eye on this young girl that hung out at the pizza place. I called her Terry Green because she always wore this green wool winter coat. She was the cutest little Italian girl, new to the neighborhood. I did get the nerve to ask her out, and eventually, we did go out for a short while. I was not really sure what happened; I knew I was pretty selfish with my time in those days, between working out, working, and hanging with my friends. She was definitely a sweetheart. In those days, everyone seemed to have a nickname. Another girl in that area named Terry had this big high-teased hairdo, and we called her Terry Head.

From the Triangle to the pizza place was about one mile. Big Davy, Joey Jet, Flash, the Mick, Jimmy D, and I headed to Joe's for a hot piece of pizza and had a nice little run to keep us warm. We ran west straight down Linden Boulevard and made a left on Van Siclen Avenue, but when we turned the corner on to Van Siclen Avenue, we stopped. Halfway down the block, there in front of the pizza place, there were about twelve bros. As we got closer, we could see that they were watching two white chicks duke it out. The bros were grabbing and inappropriately touching the girls as they fought.

As we got even closer, there was a white guy running in to break the girls up from fighting. As he was breaking them up, he said, "Don't give these motherfuckers a show." I had seen this guy around; he hung out with Johnny Reb and the Rebels.

The Rebels were a white gang in East New York; they hung out on Blake Avenue. They were a nice bunch of guys that allied with us, and we all knew that if he was good enough to hang out with the Rebels, he was good enough for us. Johnny Reb was one of those tough Irish guys you did not want to fuck with one-on-one. Most of the Rebels were young Jewish guys from Brownsville or East New York, and I would trust any of them to watch my back.

One of the Chaplains jumped in, and he and Arnie went at it. Arnie was quick, and he could bang with both hands; it didn't take him long to dispose of this guy. Another Chaplain jumped in. Arnie caught this dude with a straight right hand, knocking him on his ass. I was impressed. As we got right up to the action, we watched but knew what was going to go down. There was this one big bad ass-looking Chaplain, with his full-length Kelly green leather coat and his Marcel hair do. He turned, looked at us, and said, "Do any of you fag Jew boys want some of this?" as he raised his right fist. The bros would go to that section of East New York and fuck with the white kids there and get away with it, but not this night. Big Davy looked at me and said, "What do you think, Q?" I said, "This Rebel is kicking ass. Let's see what happens." Arnie was still kicking ass when all the Chaplains rushed in, ignoring us fag Jew boys. They threw him against a wall. At that split second, we ran in. I grabbed the big guy, spun him around, threw him up against the front bumper of a car, holding him down and punching him till he was done. He never got a shot in. All our guys were right in there; Big Davy was destroying every one he punched. Now mind you, Big Davy was six feet two, two hundred and thirty pounds, and could knock you out with his left or right hand. He was a soft-spoken guy with a street heart you could depend on. Davy lived in Cypress Hills Housing Project. The rooms in his apartment were very small. His bedroom was about ten by ten feet.

We would push his bed and furniture to one side of the room and would commence to punch the shit out of each other till his mom would throw us out. Some nights, we would go to his grandmother's (Buby) house on Wynona Street. We would go down to her cellar and continue to kick the shit out of each other. After I knocked out the big guy, I picked up a cinder block from a construction site next to the pizza place. Guys like the Mick or Joey Jet didn't have the weight, but they had the heart to stick. I'd rather have the heart any day; you knew they were there. I saw the Mick was having trouble, so I ran up to him and cracked his bro in the head with the cinder block, knocking him out facedown, eliminating his problem. Now my adrenaline was flowing. I continued banging out bros and splitting heads. By this time, the bros that could run had gone and left their people lying on the pavement. I guess they ran back to Canarsie and Brownsville. It looked like a war zone. There were about eight bros lying in the middle of the street. Arnie had this big old black eye. He was astonished. He had no idea where we came from or who we were. When his head cleared, he saw that we were the New Lots Boys. He was jumping for joy and began hugging us. He was so happy. We didn't get to have our pizza figuring someone might have called the cops. Arnie came back to New Lots Avenue with us. I told him, "With the set of balls you have, you belong with the New Lots Boys."

A week later, Big Davy suggested he and I go to the Jewish YMHA on Linden Boulevard and Van Siclen Avenue, just north, across Linden Boulevard from George Gershwin JR High School. We would go to the Y and bang the heavy bag for a while. We hit the bag for about an hour and then went downstairs where they had pool tables. We were just into our first game when we heard "Hey, Jew boys." We were playing next to an open window. There were two bros a level above us, looking down and still yelling "Motherfuckin' Jew boys." A couple of the guys in the pool room told us that these guys had been there every night this week fuckin' with them and that they would rob the coats off some of the kids that were leaving. I said, "They won't be here tomorrow night." I looked at Davy and said, "Can I be a Jew for tonight?" We went up the stairs and out the front door. They were laughing when we walked up to them. Davy put out his right hand and said, "How you doin', bro?" When the bro went to shake his hand, still laughing, Davy grabbed his hand, pulled him closer, and then threw two quick straight left hands, knocking him out. His buddy turned and ran. I went after him and caught up with him and grabbed him by the back of his coat. He ran right out of it! At first, I was a little disappointed he got away. Then I looked and saw I had his new coat in my hands. I felt better. I knew that to a bro, loosing that new coat was worse than getting a beating. After all, their favorite past time was stealing coats off fag white boys. I would have liked to have been a fly on his wall that night.

On our way back to New Lots Avenue, I saw this old Puerto Rican guy with this shabby short jacket, walking slowly and freezing his ass off. I said, "Here, Popi, this will keep you warm." I helped him off with his jacket and helped him put on this new three quarter navy blue P coat. He gave me a big smile and said, "Gracias!" I said, "De nada." We got back to New Lots and went to the terminal restaurant for a hot chocolate.

A man cannot escape the force of action by abstaining from actions! No one exists for even an instant without performing action! However unwilling, every being is forced to act by the qualities of his own nature. I remember walking home that night and feeling so alive and thinking, I only have two choices: honor or disgrace. A quote from Mr. Reginald Nero in a letter he wrote to me in 1959.

New Lots Boy versus
Harris the Giant

It was 1965 My knowledge of the world in 1965, with the newspapers and TV media and their biases, was limited. Growing up in East New York, with my parents and Mr. Nero as my conscience, taught me the difference between right and wrong. In those days, you were required to get a draft card at eighteen. I got mine, and two years later I was drafted.

In the New York City area, the government sent you a draft notice with a one-way train token to Whitehall Street in lower Manhattan. I never used the train token; my father drove me to Whitehall Street. There was a bus waiting for the new draftees to take us to Fort Dix in South Jersey. My friends Sandy and Vinnie worked across the Street from Whitehall Street and the bus stop and, with my dad, had come to see me off. This part of my life changed me forever. Basic training at Fort Dix was for eight weeks. I had no idea where Vietnam was, and I had never been farther east than New Jersey. In those days when your country called, most of us went; it was that simple. My uncles had gone before me in World War II, and they all had the same advice, "Don't volunteer!" As much as I liked to work, in the army, it was a good idea not to volunteer. It always led to some bullshit job and no appreciation.

As soon as you got off the bus, you knew you were in a world of shit. Half a dozen sergeants ran up to us, cursing, screaming, and yelling. That was OK with me as long as they didn't touch. I was assigned to Company U (Uniform Company). I found training easy enough. I was young and in great shape. Fort Dix was cold in October, November, and December, and just like in high school, there were those guys who believed they had to be bad asses, mostly the bros. The white guys would hang out with one or two other guys, while the bros hung together in large numbers and would fuck with whitey when it was convenient. It was another world when they had the numbers. I was like every other white dude; I made one or two friends in my platoon. This one cold morning, we got up early. It was still dark out. After we got inspected by Sergeant Leonard, our drill sergeant, a buff little black guy in great shape, who, by the end of basic training, I had a great respect for, he had us file out for breakfast in the main mess hall. I was among the first five guys into the mess hall. There was a mess sergeant standing in the entrance. As we walked in one by one, he told the first five of us to man the chow line. He assigned us to a post as servers behind the chow line. I was assigned to hand out toast. Young trainees are pretty hungry all the time. When a trainee got to my post and wanted two or three pieces of toast, I obliged. After a few times of obliging the trainees, the sergeant yelled in my ear, scaring the shit out of me "Trainee! If you give out more than one piece of toast per trainee, I'm putting you on KP [kitchen patrol]!" Not a good job, and I'm proud to say I always got out of ever doing KP. I yelled back, "Yes, Sergeant!" After that, I gave out one piece of toast to each trainee, and no one complained until this big ass bro stopped in front of me. I put one piece of toast on his tray. He didn't move. I said, "Can I help you?" He looked down at me and said, with this low deep tone, "I want two more pieces of toast, boy!" Not that I was afraid of the big ass dude and his muscular shoulders, I just thought, like the gentleman that I am, that it may be healthier if I explained to him what the sergeant had told me. So I did. Again he looked down at me and said, "Look, you little motherfucker, I said put two more pieces of toast on my motherfucking tray." And, like the gentleman that I am, I said, "Take a walk, scumbag." This dude looked at me like he wanted to rip out my spinal cord. He walked slowly away without a word.

Separating the chow line from the mess hall was an eight-foot-high lattice fence with a few plastic flowers and vines that basket weave through the lattice. He walked around and from the mess hall side of the lattice looked through and told me that he fucked my mother last night. This I couldn't turn inward. I have only one choice, and that is to damage this piece of shit; just for the lack of respect, thinking that this little white boy was an easy mark. His name was Harris, and he was a platoon leader for another platoon, a spit-shine dude, with sharp creased fatigues, shiny brass buckles, and spit-shine boots, and he could run the eight-minute mile in four or five minutes. I ran it in just under eight minutes. After breakfast, we went to field training, then lunch in the field. I ate light and trained light for the rest of the day. My friend Rick Roland asked me if anything was wrong and said not to let that big asshole fuck with my head. He started to say something but stopped and didn't finish. I knew what he was thinking and so was I, and it was cutting across my mind, that this dude just may kick my ass. Mr.

Nero once told me as a young man, "Everything you saw me do that took courage was to deny fear." I have lived by this all my life, and it became a steadfast rule of my life. At the end of the day, we marched back to the mess hall for dinner. Sergeant Leonard told us before falling us out that later that night, at 7:00 p.m., we had a meeting and training film in the barracks across the street, ground floor. I told the guys in my squad that I had business to take care of and asked them if they could cover for me at the meeting. Everyone in my squad, even the black guys, told me not to get into it with Harris. The black guys all heard he was a bad ass motherfucker in Harlem. (I'm not on New Lots anymore.) I knew from my street wars that very few big guys, especially the big guys that look intimidating, really get into street wars. Ninety-nine percent of the population will walk away from this visual intimidation, feeling helpless and beat. There is that 1 percent that will damage you. The only advantages I had over this dude was hopefully he had never experienced real street wars and that he took me lightly. My platoon fell out, and everyone went straight to the mess hall.

In Fort Dix, the barracks were new three-story buildings, brick on the outside and painted cinder block walls on the inside, VA tile floor, with two, four, six, and eight man rooms. Another big advantage I would have bet on was that Harris ate like a pig. Mr. Nero once told me a story about when he was in the army that there was this big nasty fat white sergeant that would fuck with him daily. Mr. Nero, being a private first class and not a very big guy, never said a word, until this fat piece of shit, taking Mr. Nero for granted, told Mr. Nero to meet him at night behind the barracks. Mr. Nero knew this fat fuck would eat like a pig. Mr. Nero didn't go to dinner; he went behind the barracks, sucked on a piece of candy, and waited. The Sergeant came with a couple of guys as the sun was going down. They were laughing and pointing, as the sergeant got closer, calling Mr. Nero his little nigger. Mr. Nero gave this shithead a right-hand punch in his fat ass belly. He hit the floor gasping for air and vomiting. Mr. Nero, like the gentleman that he is, just walked away without a word (the art of listening). I went up to my room, took a shower, put on a pair of new starched fatigue pants, a light cotton sweatshirt, and a pair of spit-shine boots. I was in a two-man room, and Harris was in an eight man room. I sucked on a piece of candy and went to Harris's room. He had the end bunk close to the window. This trainee I knew from East New York, Walter, was in the hallway. I asked if he could warn me when Harris was coming and if he was with his bros, could he tell them to wait outside and that I would like to talk to him. Walter knew me and knew this was going to be a war. I could see the pride and admiration in him when he said, "You still have that East New York head." I knew I only had a few minutes before Harris would get to his room. I was hungry and that was a good thing; I loosened up till I broke a sweat. I didn't need Walter to tell me when Harris and his entourage were headed up; I could hear them from across the road. I stood next to Harris's bunk; one foot on the floor and my other foot on his perfectly made bed. I was one hundred and sixty-five pounds, young and lean, and I had been training for this since I was twelve years old. I had my battle scars. I couldn't have been more ready.

The door to the entrance of the room was half open, and the next thing I saw and heard was the door being kicked completely open, banging against the block wall with a loud bang. I stood straight up. Harris walked straight toward me with at least ten bros behind him. As he kept moving forward, he was saying with a voice monotonously flat, "Do you want to talk to me, boy?" I said, "Ya. Either you apologize or throw up your hands." As he got even closer, he said, "Apologize to a little shit like you?" As he got close enough, I climbed him like a big oak tree and held him by the neck with my left hand, trying to bring him down while banging him with six-inch right hands. He lifted me off the ground and tried slamming me against the cinder block walls, at the same time trying to rip me off him. I held tight and close enough to him so that he couldn't get off any shots. I remember reading a story about Joe Louis having a devastating six-inch punch, and I trained for years throwing short inside right hands. He tried to throw a few right hands and did catch me with three shots to the left side of my face, but they had no effect, and I was focused and never stopped banging. Harris collapsed under the nonstop fire power, a steady stream of right hands; he went down and fell onto a bunk and slid down to the hard cold tile floor. The bros were in shock! You could hear a pin drop. If I had learned anything from all my wars in East New York, it was that I must take his heart. The bros are now yelling that he had had enough. I lifted his limp body up, leaned him against the wall, held him with my left hand by his chin and neck, and threw straight right hands, breaking his ribs, arm, and head and knocking out his top front teeth. The bros were still yelling. I stopped and he slid down to the floor. I turned and looked at this sorry crew and said, "Now he has had enough." It happened so quickly with this ugly physical effect, maybe they figured it would be better not to get involved with someone they really didn't know that well. I walked back through the small group that gathered, walked down the hall, and went back into my room. I was drenched with blood. I grabbed a T-shirt and some fresh starched fatigues, headed for the latrine, and washed up. I had my own little white entourage following me and patting me on my back. I got dressed and went downstairs and across the street to where my platoon was having their meeting. The lights were out, and everyone was watching this training film. I tried to sneak in without being heard or seen. As soon as I sat down, the projector shut off and the lights went on. I had grabbed a seat in the back of the room. Sergeant Leonard looked at me and said, "Stand up, Quarantello, and tell us what happened." I stood up. Now the whole class was staring at me; my fatigues were sharp, and the three shots Harris hit me with didn't show yet. Apparently, everyone in the room knew what was going down, even Sergeant Leonard. I'm sure from my appearance that it looked to them like I was never in a war. Sergeant Leonard said again, "We're waiting! What happened with Harris?" I said, "I did what I do best, Sergeant." It was dark out and cold. Everyone turned when they heard a siren and looked out the window through the now open venetian blinds. There in the night sky, you could see the colored lights from the base ambulance that had just stopped in front of my barracks. Right on cue, everyone turned and looked back at me. I expected that night or by the next morning the military police would come to arrest me. But they didn't, and a week went by without a word. Trainees from Harris's platoon were coming up to me on the firing range and shaking my hand, telling me how grateful they were and that he was such a prick and a bully, still not believing that a little guy like me did all that damage. Another week went by, and our basic training was over. We now were waiting for our orders and a long-awaited leave. There wasn't much to do on this one morning, so my friend Rick Roland and I went to the mess hall for breakfast. We got in at the end of the line. In front of me loomed this big bro with his arm in a sling and this turban like head bandage wrapped around his head. It had been two weeks, and I never gave it a thought that this guy was Harris. I was talking with Rick when this guy steps out of the line and walks to the back of the line. That was when Rick looked at me and said, "Do you know that guy in front of us was Harris?" I guess it should have felt good, but it didn't. I didn't like the thought of breaking another man's spirit. I never saw or heard from the man again. I got my orders to go to Fort Gordon GA for advanced infantry training (AIT), with a twenty-one day much needed leave. I was going home to my family, friends, and the loveliest young lady I've ever known, the cutest little half Irish, half Italian girl who I was dating before I went into the service, Patty H. Rick Roland lived in the Bronx, and we decided to get tickets to a play in New York and take our girlfriends. I had the greatest night; we went to see *Golden Boy* with Sammy Davis Jr. and Lola Falana on Broadway, and afterward, we went to dinner at the famous restaurant Momma Leones. By this time, I knew where Vietnam was; and with all the news coverage, I knew this was not good. My relationship with Patty didn't last because it was possible that I might not come back. I didn't see the sense in her worrying, and I had seen how guys in basic training worried about their girlfriends. Guys would break other guy's balls by telling them how "Joedi" was doing their girlfriends. Patty was too nice a girl for me to ever believe that. I knew at this young age I needed a clear head and that this war was real. I needed to free her and myself from the "what if." I preferred that she carried the relationship loss. Let me tell you, the reader, how I feel about this story. I never felt any hate at any time for Harris. I listened, I learned, and I was ready and battle tested. I do know one thing about the man; when his country called, he went, and that alone makes me proud of the man, and if he was called to watch my back, I have no doubt he would have. (Soldiers don't start wars! Governments do! And they employ us to do the dying!) Soldier, you are the backbone of your nation. (God bless America.)

NEW LOTS BOY VERSUS COMPANY BROS

It was 1966. My first time on an airplane. I flew from New York LaGuardia Airport to Atlanta, Georgia. After my leave in New York and after doing basic training at Fort Dix, my orders were to go to Fort Gordon in Augusta GA for AIT training. I reported in on a weekend. Then on Monday, I was assigned to Company C (Charlie Company). We were put in the old wooden barracks with one large room upstairs, a large room downstairs, and a small room where the drill Sergeant slept. Each floor had at least twenty or more bunk beds. By late December, it had started to get pretty cold in Georgia with a few snow flurries. I remember feeling bad for the new trainees at Fort Dix; if it was cold here, it had to be freezing in New Jersey. Their saving grace was that they had hot running water all the time in their new Barracks. We were in the old style wooden building, with no insulation and an old potbelly stove to heat the water; so 99 percent of the time, we showered with cold water. I did what I had to do to stay clean. My hygiene was always very important to me. Things were going pretty good. I had made a couple of friends, one of them was Wetzel, from Howard Beach, Queens, just east on the border line of East New York. This one morning, at 4:00 a.m., we had to fall out for inspection, then to breakfast, then to the field for training, with starched fatigues, spit-shine boots, and brass buckle shining without a scratch and right on your gig line. (Gig line was the left side of your brass buckle lined up with the zipper of your fatigue pants.) I always did pretty well in this area. It was dark and cold, it was uncomfortable, and we were always tired. We were outside in formation waiting for our sergeant and captain to inspect us before we went to breakfast when a fight broke out between Wetzel and this black guy from the Bronx. Wetzel was getting the best of this dude when another Bro jumped in and kicked Wetzel in the head, knocking him off.

Again, without thinking, I ran in and punched this dude to the ground. I saw Wetzel get up and split. Bros were all over me now. I was backing up and throwing punches and the bros were all over me, trying to get to me, when I felt bros being ripped off me. I was still banging, and there were a few bros laid out, but now they backed off, and I stepped back. Standing shoulder to shoulder next to me was this skinny Irish-looking dude. We looked at each other, and I said, "Thanks, man." He shook my hand and said, "Where the fuck did you come from, Superman?" On the ground, there were three bros laid out and one guy standing and yelling that that white motherfucker broke his nose. Now, standing in front of us like weeds rustling in the darkness were dozens of bros. I looked at my new bad ass Irish buddy and the closeness of his presence. I said, "This doesn't look healthy." He said, "Let's do it!" This reminded me of my friends on New Lots Avenue. Now, giving and taking became one. My only choice remaining was to meet my fear. No one was stepping forward. All I could hear was yelling and cursing at us white punk motherfuckers. My new buddy was yelling back, "Let's do it, man!" I was amused by his indifference. Running out of the captain's building were the first sergeant, the captain, and the first lieutenant, screaming for us to fall in. Everyone jumped back into formation and stood at attention. They were still screaming "What the fuck is going on?" when this bro with the broken nose jumped out, yelling and pointing at me and my new Mick friend. (A Mick is an Irish dude, which was a term of endearment to me.) I never met an Irishman without spirit. The captain yelled at us to get out of formation and double time to his office, which we did. We stood at attention in front of his desk. We had name tags on our fatigue shirts. The captain yelled, "Kevany! What's the problem?" They knew him. He was one of the stars on their basketball team, and this Irish dude knew all the bros. I was astonished! This guy had courage, and I was so proud, and he spoke to the Captain like they were old buddies. They had the company now fall out for breakfast. The first sergeant looked at us and said, "Tommy [that was the first time I heard my new friend's first name], what the fuck are you two thinking?" I said, "First Sergeant, Tommy was just trying to break it up; he had nothing to do with this." I didn't want him to get into trouble. The captain looked at me and said "So what the hell were you thinking?" "Sergeant! I wasn't thinking. I was reacting. The first sergeant said, "Don't be a wise guy." I said, "I don't have a problem with these guys, but they seem to have a problem with me, so please don't ask me to take their shit." I was very surprised to hear the captain say, "I do understand, and if there is another episode with these guys, come and see me. I'll take care of it. Now fall out and go to breakfast." "Yes, Sergeant!" and Tommy and I were gone. We laughed all the way to the mess hall. When we opened the doors to the mess hall, everyone stopped talking. We only had about fifteen minutes to get chow, so we doubled time to the chow line and got a few dirty looks on our way. We ate without incident and had to fall out for training. A couple of guys came up to me during the day and wanted to know if I needed help with those dudes. I thanked them. It was nice to know I had some backup. Except for the morning, the rest of the day was non-eventful. Tommy was an all-star basketball player in Bensonhurst Brooklyn. He knew most of the bros, and they weren't very happy with him. He was so indifferent about the situation with his I don't give a shit attitude. Tommy came up to me early that evening and told me that the bros had this white dude they looked up to, a Greek guy from Detroit who was tall with dark brown eyes and a dark olive complexion. Tommy was told that he was going to fuck me up after lights out. I told Tommy, "If this dude doesn't do a good job on me, revenge is sweet, and it will be mine." Next thing I knew, I was waking up in the morning to our platoon sergeant blowing this loud brass whistle. It was still dark out. We got dressed, and the sergeant ordered us to police up the cigarette butts in the back of our barracks. Tommy and I were cursing the sergeant for getting us up extra early to do this shit; Tommy didn't smoke, and neither did I. We were picking up butts when this Greek dude walked past us with this cold and ugly stare. I had no tolerance for this and having had to worry about sleeping at night and being caught defenseless. This dude was looking right through me when I said, "Yo, you got a problem with me?" At first, he didn't say a word. I said, "Dude, if you've got something to say or do, do it now like a man." He said, "What's your problem, motherfucker?" I said, "You!" This guy was now jive talking me like a bro; I didn't even understand half of what he was saying. I said, "What the fuck are you saying? Is that English?" (I was from East New York, Brooklyn, and I could pretty much mess up the King's English, but I think you could understand me.) He looked at me with this big smile on his face and said, "You've got balls, talking to me like that. I'm from Detroit." I liked the guy. It seemed the bros looked up to him, and he wasn't backing off. I think he was a little confused by my aggression. We stopped dogging each other and began talking. We became friends, and the Greek (Kentros), Tommy, one of the black guys (Holbrook), one of the guys that said he would watch my back, and I started a doo-wop group. We did songs like "Mickey's Monkey" by the Miracles and "Sometimes When I'm All Alone'" by Danny and the Juniors. So for a short time, we did our thing. I never had a problem again. Most of the bros just wanted to know when we were going to sing. The sad part was we were too naive and living in the moment to understand our near future.

NEW LOTS BOY VERSUS THE NEW WAR

At the end of AIT, we were put on a bus and shipped from Fort Gordon to Fort Benning Georgia and four weeks of jump school. I now had a little bit of a reputation, so I think between that and knowing by now where we would all be heading, all us young bloods pretty much stayed in check. I went from jump school on leave to New York. After my stay in New York, I took a plane out of LaGuardia airport to Oakland, California, were I stayed for three weeks waiting for orders to be shipped to Vietnam. While on leave, one weekend in San Francisco, I met this cute young lady named Cathy; and for the next couple of weekends, I had a great time and the perfect send off with this lovely young lady. I was shipped out to Vietnam. I was placed with the 101st Airborne Division 2/502 Recon. In one month, my whole world changed. I volunteered to be point man. It was the only position where you didn't think of home and stayed alert. Being brought up in New York City, I didn't know the jungle. I did, by this time, know that my instincts were sharp, as I had been handed a rope most of my life, my benediction. My joy of life was cut short when I killed my first two men in 1966. Company C was overrun by Vietcong (VC). We were forced to march through the jungle all night in monsoon rains. We got to where the battle was at dawn. The battle was over when we came up to where the main battle had been. There were dead VC and GIs everywhere. My head was spinning. It all became so real. Next thing I heard was laughing. I walked right up on three VC and opened up on automatic with my M16, killing one VC out of the three. The other two split. I had emptied a twenty-round magazine. That was the very last time I ever used automatic again. When I realized that my ammo magazine was empty, I fumbled to change a new magazine. Not three or four feet in front of me, I saw the earth move. Instinctively, I opened fire on that position, on semiautomatic. Again, the earth moved. This time a hand came out of a spider hole (small hole in the ground that housed one man, covered by camouflage). I ran up to the area, lifted the top halfway off a spider hole, and dropped a grenade inside, dropped the top, and stepped back. I wasn't proud. I had just killed two people I didn't know, halfway around the world. Would their kinsmen grieve? They didn't threaten my family, friends, neighborhood, or country. It made no sense to me. East New York was in a desperate battle, a loss of moral order. After that day, I knew right there that my blind faith and free will were lost. I did the rest of my tour in Vietnam in survival mode, eager to get home. From that time on, my journey was to seek inner peace and purpose. It was my privilege to have served my country and an honor to have done so with brave young men like Tommy Kevaney. (He died in 1967 on a three man outpost in Vietnam. He served with the proud 173 Airborne Division. I bear a heavy burden of sorrow.) I needed to find my place in the world again.

Richie Q—Tatoo of my three Purple Hearts
God Bless America

INDEX

S

S., Anthony, 49, 123, 161
S., Lillian, 42, 116
S., Richie, 39–40, 61, 70
S., Stevie, 121–23, 125, 165, 167–68
Saigon, 163
Saint Gabriel Rectory, 49
Saints, 102–5
Sal, 19, 80, 145, 148–49
Sammy, 164
Sandy, 58–59, 61, 117–18, 173
Schenck Avenue, 108–9
Schermerhorn Street, 19
Schmidt mobile, 102–3, 105, 146–47, 167
Schmitty, 58, 102, 167
Scotty, 119
Sergeant Leonard, 174–75, 177
Seventh-Fifth Precinct, 56, 58
Sheila, 162–63
Shelly, 166–67
Snail, 133
Soldiers, 178
Sonny, 19, 35, 40, 42, 55–56, 58–62, 64–65, 110, 135–38, 161
Stephanie, 161
Steve, 58, 60–61, 121, 165
St. Fortunata, 57, 141
Stitt, Sonny, 138
street crusades, 33, 56
street games, 115
street gangs, 13, 165
street warfare, 28, 30, 37, 104, 110, 175
Sutter Avenue, 41, 69–71, 117, 146, 153

T

Thomson Street, 138
Tommy, 34, 50, 125, 163, 180–81

Tony, 18, 28, 80, 108, 110, 113, 156–60, 163
trainees, 174–75, 177
Triangle, 13, 24, 28, 41, 44, 51–52, 55, 62, 66, 69–71, 104, 117, 122, 131, 135–37, 141–42, 144–46, 148, 150, 152, 158–59, 167, 169

U

Uncle Frank, 13–14, 20, 43, 48, 66, 110, 140, 153
Uncle Tom, 125–26

V

Van Siclen Avenue, 169
Vietnam, 13, 76, 90–93, 104, 161, 163, 173, 177, 182–83

W

Walter, 80, 89, 175–76
Warwick Street, 111
watchman, 161
Wetzel, 179–80
whistle, 12
White Castle, 122–23
white gangs, 13, 59, 106, 114, 145, 162, 170
Whitehall Street, 173
Wiseguy, 62
Wynona Street, 170

Z

Zippo, 52

About the Author

I was born on February 6, 1945, to Josephine and Dominick Quarantello in Brooklyn, New York, into a second-generation Italian American.

I went to PS 202, East New York, Brooklyn, in grade school and East New York Vocational and Thomas Jefferson in high school. At the age of sixteen years, I'd left school to begin working, first as a butcher then as a carpet installer.

In the year 1965, I was drafted at the age of twenty years, sent to Vietnam, and wounded three times, receiving three Purple Hearts. After Vietnam, I married, had three children, and became an entrepreneur in the carpet business. Years later, I retired to Florida then relocated to Costa Rica.

I relocated to Costa Rica with my wife to begin a new journey—writing my autobiography, rescuing animals, and performing music with local Latin and reggae bands, in which I was a vocalist and played saxophone and flute.

I am currently living in Florida, performing music, completing my autobiography, working on a sequel, and living the best life I possibly can with no regrets and no apologies.